48 Answers

for

My Son

An Architecture of Integrated Leadership Intelligence

Costantino Delli

Published by COS™ Books

Reader reflections, feedback, or media inquiries are welcome: BooksbyCOS@gmail.com

The cover photograph is a portrait of the author, taken in the midst of his journey—the cities that shaped his life appear as a living backdrop: Taranto, where the story began; New York, Hollywood, and the world beyond. The image captures a moment of witnessing—a man becoming aware of the life he is living, standing behind it with clarity, and passing forward a legacy that continues to unfold.

Delli, Costantino

48 Answers for My Son: An Architecture of Integrated Leadership Intelligence

ISBN: 978-0-9796237-4-5 (Paperback)

ISBN: 978-0-9796237-5-2 (eBook)

Registration No. TXu 2-541-215

Printed in the United States of America

Costantino Delli, age one—Taranto, Italy

DEDICATION

For the boy I was at eight,

who left one world without knowing why,

and carried questions he didn't yet have answers for.

For the man shaped by experience—

work, love, loss, faith, and renewal—

who lived those moments wholeheartedly.

And for the man I am today,

who can look back with gratitude,

stand fully behind the life he has lived,

and who is ready for the next movie of his life.

Gratitude

Gratitude is the foundation of my living philosophy.

My mother—for her tenacity, courage, and unending love for her family. She was my first true leader. Through her strength and perseverance, she showed me how to endure with dignity and love without condition.

My father—complex on the surface, yet profoundly beautiful within. I always knew who he truly was. I honor the depth of his soul and carry my love for him quietly and forever.

My brother—whose early love and support shaped me in ways that remain part of who I am.

My Italian family—my roots, my memories, my living history, and lifelong friends whom I hold close and proudly call my Italian family.

My friends—thank you for the seasons of growth, the laughter, and the becoming.

Intimate relationships—for the shared joy, the love, and the moments that shaped my emotional landscape and deepened my humanity.

Colleagues in the corporate world—for inspiring discipline, excellence, and aspiration through shared work and high standards.

My clients—for the trust of partnership, the privilege of responsibility, and the shared pursuit of meaningful results.

Organizations and communities I have supported and served—for the opportunity to contribute, grow, and align around shared values.

I hold special gratitude for individuals whose leadership, creativity, and example left a lasting imprint on me:

Mike Bloomberg, Jamie Dimon, Sherry Lansing, Deepak Chopra, Julia Cameron, Sande Shurin, Lilyan Chauvin, Simon Cooper, and Bill Marriott—for the spirit of service and enduring legacy they represent.

The Ritz-Carlton Gold Standards—a philosophy of service and excellence that deeply resonates with my own values. And Arne Sorenson—whose humanity, grace, and living example of leadership remain a quiet standard I carry forward.

I also offer gratitude to the precious animals who shared my life and taught me presence in ways only they could:

Bianco, my Pekingese, who showed me how to live fully in the moment;

Merlin, my Russian Blue, who accompanied me through the writing of my first book;

and Mahi-Mahi, whose quiet companionship continues to bring steadiness and grace.

And my deepest gratitude to Apple—for the beautiful years we shared, for the love, laughter, magical moments, and dreams that filled them.

TABLE OF CONTENTS

Introduction

After writing *The Way: Live Your Dream, It's Not a Secret!* (now evolved into *Creative Optimum Self: Transform Your Life and Your World)*, I believed the work was complete. That book captured a set of principles I had lived by long before I formally shared them in writing—principles grounded in awareness, responsibility, and inner coherence. What I didn't anticipate was what would happen after it was written.

I began to see those same ideas reflected back to me everywhere: in conversations, in leadership discourse, in social dialogue, and in the lives of people navigating their own turning points. It felt less like influence and more like recognition—as if something I had lived was part of a broader, unseen current already moving through the world. What I did not expect was that the act of writing this book would quietly awaken that earlier work.

As I began shaping these questions and answers, reflecting on my life, I felt naturally drawn back to my first book. In revisiting it, I saw an opportunity to update and refine it in light of how my thinking and philosophy had evolved over the years. Together, these two works now form a natural continuum: *Creative Optimum Self*, which explores the foundations of **Integrated Being Intelligence**, and *48 Answers for My Son*, which reflects the lived practice of **Integrated Leadership Intelligence**—two complementary volumes of the same evolving philosophy.

Beneath all of this, I had carried another idea quietly: to one day share the story of my life. Not as a traditional memoir, but as a reflection on how a life unfolds—through questions, choices, ruptures, and renewal. I had shared pieces of that story privately with people I respected deeply, Robert Redford and Sherry Lansing, both of whom encouraged the clarity and honesty of my voice. Still, the timing never felt right.

That changed on the fifth anniversary of my mother's passing. In that stillness, something settled into clarity, and I chose a simple structure: forty-eight sequential questions, each unfolding as a scene from my life—followed by reflection and distilled takeaways. Read in order, they trace a life as if you were watching a film, where each moment builds upon the last and meaning gradually reveals itself through lived consequence. And in that realization, something became clear: this book is a transmission—an offering drawn from the life I have lived and the leadership that life itself revealed.

This book serves three essential purposes. It continues the philosophy introduced in *Creative Optimum Self* through lived practice. It offers a high-level arc of my life—its acceleration, collapse, integration, and renewal. And it stands as a message to a future son, a future self, or anyone drawn to understanding how a human life can be lived with awareness, integrity, and coherence.

I chose a Q&A format because it allows the story to unfold as life itself does—through questions that arise along the way. Presented in chronological sequence, each question marks a moment that had to be faced, understood, and integrated. Each answer reflects a lived experience—moments that shaped understanding and carried life forward. Read together, they reveal a life unfolding scene by scene, where each moment builds upon the last and meaning gradually comes into focus. This book is a record of becoming.

If you are reading this as my son, know that everything here was written with love, honesty, and respect for your own path. Use it as a guide for reflection, allowing your own path to unfold.

If you are reading this as another version of me, remember what it took to arrive here.

And if you are reading this simply as a fellow traveler, may these pages meet you wherever you are along your own path.

A Note on the Architecture

Beneath the reflections and lived experiences shared in these pages is a deeper architecture—one that gradually became visible as I looked back across the arc of my life. Over time, patterns of awareness, decision-making, and responsibility revealed themselves as interdependent dimensions of intelligence expressed both inwardly and outwardly.

At the foundation is Integrated Being Intelligence—the inward integration of Source, mind, body, emotions, and relationships. These dimensions shape how a human being experiences life from the inside: how awareness forms, how meaning is interpreted, and how coherence is cultivated within one's own existence.

From this inward coherence emerges Integrated Leadership Intelligence—the outward expression of that same alignment as it moves into the world. Here, the dimensions take form through Source, cognition, emotions, the social field of human interaction, and the cultural environments in which leadership unfolds. Both expressions arise from the same origin—the Creative Optimum Self—an inner Source from which clarity, responsibility, and purposeful action naturally emerge.

The forty-eight answers that follow trace this unfolding through lived experience. Each moment on the page reflects a real encounter with life—moments of acceleration, rupture, reflection, and renewal. After each scene, a brief reflection offers perspective and context, allowing the reader to observe how understanding gradually takes shape. The questions are arranged chronologically allowing the reader to move through life as it was lived—scene by scene—allowing meaning to accumulate naturally through experience.

The key takeaways distill what was quietly forming beneath each moment, revealing how leadership develops long before it carries a title. As the journey progresses, coherence strengthens, choices sharpen, and Integrated Leadership Intelligence emerges as the natural expression of a life lived with awareness. I offer this journey as it unfolded.

May it remind us how deeply connected we are in our shared humanity.

Author's Note

Thank you for picking up this book.

It chronicles my life—from being born in beautiful Taranto, Italy many years ago, to the present day.

I believe that when we step back and look at our lives through the lens of a camera, every life becomes a movie. Over the years, many have shared with me that mine has been unique and compelling. I have lived it fully, capturing it across thousands of journal pages. In our humanity we experience joy, rupture, ambition, fear, love, responsibility, and reinvention. Beneath our different circumstances, we share far more than we sometimes realize.

When I considered how to share my life, I wanted the structure of this book to reflect who I am—both inwardly and in the world. I am analytical and creative. Structured and intuitive. Grounded in mathematics and science, yet shaped by hospitality, service, and storytelling. Looking back, the experiences of my life can be viewed as a series of moments that shaped direction, responsibility, and growth. Each answer in this book is written as a scene drawn from a lived moment. In many ways, these scenes can be read as case studies in Integrated Leadership Intelligence, observing experience with clarity and engagement. Then I step back.

The Reflections offer context around what was happening beneath the surface. They name patterns, pressures, and internal shifts that are often invisible while we are living them. The Key Takeaways distill a lifetime of lived leadership—one that began unannounced at five years old. It has always been present. Long before titles, leadership showed up as responsibility, protection, discipline, sacrifice, and repair.

Over time, I learned to translate experience into principle—to learn, improve, and evolve. At times, the Reflections may revisit similar themes, as patterns often repeat until a lesson is integrated. The Key Takeaways accumulate over time, revealing the arc of Integrated Leadership Intelligence.

Everything in this book is true to my lived experience and memory. I share it as if speaking to my son, a friend, or a chronicler of truth—recounting my life as it unfolded. I invite you to witness what took place as if you were there in that moment.

If you've read my companion book, *Creative Optimum Self: Transform Your Life and Your World*, you'll recognize the inner and outer philosophy that guides how I live and lead. That book expresses the framework. This book reveals it through lived experience.

My hope is simple: that as you move through these scenes, you sense the quiet thread of our shared humanity. That something within these moments feels familiar—because beneath our different paths, we all experience life through the same hopes, fears, losses, and renewal.

And that you feel encouraged in your own leadership, however it shows up in your world.

This is my movie.

Forty-eight scenes revealing

how I arrived here.

CHAPTER ONE

The Way We Were

Loving Italy, Almost Dying, and Leaving Without Knowing Why

Q1

You were born in southern Italy, in Taranto, at a time when your parents operated a café—a setting rooted in routine, community, and work from an early age.

When you think back to your earliest years there, what is the first memory that comes to you—something you remember seeing, hearing, or feeling firsthand?

My first memories of growing up in Taranto come as a series of warm, overlapping images—scenes of movement, sound, and belonging.

My parents operated a neighborhood café that served coffee, pastries, and pizza on the corner of a street in the newer part of town. I remember playing outside in the streets with friends—hide-and-seek, kicking a soccer ball around the playground, or in the parking lot where a municipal building and courthouse were being constructed. That space felt like part playground, part construction site where the future was quietly taking shape.

Inside the café, I was never just a child passing time. I helped my mother prepare homemade ice cream, and I helped my father by handing change to customers. I was five years old, small enough that I had to drag a chair from inside the café to stand high enough to play the pinball machine. I remember standing there, balanced against it, completely absorbed. We lived across the street, in a first-floor apartment. The balcony overlooked the café, creating a constant visual and emotional connection between home and work. I remember family meals—day and evening—the rhythm of food, conversation, and routine. There was a sense of warmth, of continuity. We went to the beach. Life felt open, communal, alive.

That early sense of continuity ended abruptly with a life-threatening surgery—an interruption that arrived before I had language to understand it.

Reflections

This scene captures belonging before identity forms.

Home and work exist together. Play and responsibility intertwine naturally. Community is lived through faces, food, movement, and routine.

The café becomes an early classroom in attention, contribution, and awareness.

Responsibility is introduced naturally. A child hands change to customers, watches adults interact, senses rhythm and order. Participation comes before ambition.

The abrupt shift to surgery interrupts that continuity. Stability ends without explanation. The body encounters vulnerability before the mind has language for it.

Key Takeaways

1. Leadership often begins as contribution—helping before being asked.

2. Growing up inside community builds comfort with people, responsibility, and shared space.

3. Early disruption teaches the body what the mind has not yet learned: life can change suddenly.

Q2

You've just described a childhood defined by warmth, movement, and early responsibility—and then you mention a life-threatening surgery at the age of five.

What happened?

Yes, it was dramatic—and it began with blame.

I was told I had developed appendicitis because I drank cold water while I was playing outside, sweating. As a child, I absorbed that explanation simply: something I did caused this. I was taken to the hospital and operated on.

Years later, I learned what actually happened. The appendicitis itself had nothing to do with cold water. During the operation, the surgeon performing the procedure was intoxicated. During the procedure, he tied my intestine to remove the appendix—and failed to release it before closing the incision, creating a life-threatening complication. I spent three days in the hospital in critical condition. I remember lying in the bed, unable to eat or drink. My mother and my aunt were there, speaking quietly. Nurses would place ice cubes on my lips to keep them from drying out. Eventually, I was taken back into the operating room. I remember the large lamp hanging directly over the table. I stared at it, closed my eyes—and the next thing I remember is waking up in bed again.

What followed was a thirty-day hospital stay. I remember fragments from that recovery. One nurse, trying to keep my spirits up, asked if I wanted to be her boyfriend when I got out of the hospital. I remember slapping her. At the time, I did not understand why I reacted that way. I only knew something in me resisted the moment. The deeper reasons would become clearer much later.

I later learned how close I came to dying. If not for my mother's tenacity, I likely would not have survived. She was deeply Catholic. She walked several miles to a church and gave all of her gold to the Blessed Mother, praying for my life. When doctors insisted there was nothing wrong with me, she refused to accept it. She demanded intervention—and ultimately compelled a visiting doctor from Switzerland to operate on me correctly.

That experience shaped my life profoundly—my bond with my mother, my sense of survival, and the way I later approached responsibility, leadership, and care.

Reflections

This scene marks the moment survival enters identity.

Blame is absorbed before comprehension. A child internalizes fault, and over time that internalization transforms into disciplined ownership.

The mother models leadership as protection. When institutions hesitate, conviction intervenes. Authority emerges through care and conviction.

Emotion expresses itself indirectly—through resistance, silence, vigilance. Strength forms before language defines it.

This rupture establishes an early baseline: intensity, alertness, responsibility—rooted first in survival, later translated into leadership.

Key Takeaways

1. Early blame can shape identity—but it can also be redirected into personal responsibility.

2. Leadership often begins as protection: standing firm when others hesitate.

3. Experiences the body survives early in life often become the structure we rely on later.

Q3

After surviving something severe at such a young age, life doesn't simply return to where it left off—even if a child can't yet articulate that shift.

After the hospital, what do you remember being different?

Recovery did not end when I left the hospital. It followed me home.

When I was discharged, people gave me gifts. I had been there for such a long time that sympathy surrounded me. In a way, I became a kind of victim—treated gently, watched closely. I was fitted with a waist protector, almost like a bra wrapped around my stomach, to make sure everything inside healed properly. The stitches came out after a week or two, but I wore that support for much longer—close to a month. I remember how it changed my body. I walked hunched over, unable to straighten my back fully. What's strange is that even now, decades later, I sometimes catch myself doing the same thing. The body remembers.

My mother became even more protective. She would carry me around town and she wanted to give me things, to make me happy. I remember being fascinated by a watch. I wanted one badly, drawn to time without understanding why. When I tried to return to normal life, the transition was uneven. I went to kindergarten—Bambi was the name of the school. A nun approached me and offered me milk. I slapped her. It happened again—the same reaction as before. I wasn't allowed to return after that. I never finished kindergarten.

I did, however, go on to first grade. And there, something shifted. I did well. I was especially good with numbers and mathematics. I remember receiving an award for being able to count backwards. Clarity started to return. Slowly, life normalized. I was running on the beach again. I remember eating a peach on the sand, playing soccer, feeling my body come back to itself. It took about a year. By the time I was eight, life felt whole again—playful, happy, open.

And then came another dramatic change. My mother decided to take me to the United States for what was supposed to be only a visit.

Reflections

Survival leaves residue.

The body carries posture long after stitches are removed. Protection becomes environment. Sympathy slowly becomes identity.

The repeated slap reveals emotion that had no language yet—something unprocessed seeking release. Emotion often surfaces physically before language can explain it.

What stabilizes the arc is structure. Counting backward. Precision. Numbers introduce order where disruption unsettled it. The mind begins organizing what the body endured.

Recovery unfolds gradually—brace, milk, beach, movement. Strength returns in increments. Just as equilibrium settles, transition returns.

Movement begins forming as pattern.

Key Takeaways

1. The body often carries experiences long after the event has passed.

2. Extended protection can shape identity in ways that are not immediately visible.

3. When emotion feels unstable, structure can provide early stability.

Q4

You've described finally returning to a sense of normalcy in Italy—physically, emotionally, and socially—and then, at eight years old, leaving for the United States.

What was that trip supposed to be, and what did it become?

At the time, I believed the trip to the United States was just a visit. My mother's aunt had previously come from America to see us, and this felt reciprocal—temporary. I remember being reluctant to leave. I didn't want to say goodbye to my friends, my father, or my brother. I had no sense that I was stepping away from a life rather than stepping out briefly.

We missed our flight. My mother and I were stranded, and because of her graciousness—her ability to speak with warmth, conviction, and dignity—the airline went above and beyond. They put us up in a hotel in Rome. Years later, I would learn it was the Hotel Flora, a place I would return to many times as an adult. That night left an imprint on me. A tall, dark-skinned man in a crisp white uniform—elegant, handsome—was asked to look after me. He may have been a waiter or a concierge, but to me he embodied something larger: care, presence, hospitality. I had already been raised inside my parents' café; service and attentiveness were familiar—but this felt elevated. That moment aligned deeply with my mother's influence and quietly shaped my future orientation toward hospitality and service.

My father came to stay with us that night after traveling from Taranto when he learned we'd missed the flight. I was happy to have the opportunity to share more time with my father. The journey itself was painful. I wasn't happy. I cried throughout the flight. It was my first time flying, on Air India, connecting through London. I cried because I was leaving something essential behind: my home, my father, my brother, my friends, and my Taranto.

We arrived in New York on September 23. At JFK, distant cousins I had never met before picked us up in a large Cadillac. Everything felt unfamiliar. They drove us to their home in Hamilton Township, New Jersey, near Trenton.

My first impression was the landscape. Everything was flat. It was completely different from the seaside city of southern Italy where I grew up. This was America—vast, unfamiliar, and disorienting.

I did not want to be there. I wanted to go home.

Reflections

This is the first conscious experience of separation.

The departure was presented as temporary, but the body understood something more permanent. Grief surfaced midair. Change often registers emotionally before it is explained logically.

Hospitality reappears at a higher level. Service is no longer only familial—it is professional, composed, dignified. A seed is planted: care can be elevated into craft.

The mother remains the stabilizing force. Her warmth creates continuity even when geography changes.

The external world expands dramatically. The internal sense of belonging contracts.

Displacement becomes the beginning of adaptation.

Key Takeaways

1. Major change is often understood emotionally before it is understood intellectually.

2. Early encounters with dignity in service can shape long-term values and vocational direction.

3. Displacement challenges belonging—but it also expands perspective and capacity.

Q5

What do you remember most vividly about your first days in America—the sights, the sounds, the interactions?

My first impressions of America were physical before they were emotional. Everything felt big and flat. The landscape stretched outward without interruption—completely different from the seaside city in southern Italy where I had grown up. That contrast stayed with me.

My cousins welcomed us into their home. There was food waiting for us, unmistakably American. Soon after, my mother and I went to stay with my mother's aunt—my great-aunt—in Trenton. We slept on a couch that unfolded into a bed. I remember being introduced to a large television—much bigger than anything I had known—and to American talk shows. My great-aunt watched *Merv Griffin*. That name stayed with me. It was my first exposure to American voices, rhythms, and conversation.

The next day unfolded quickly. My cousin, Tony, who was a sheriff, took us out. His sister, Maybelline, owned a shoe store, and we went there together. While we were there, an Italian bakery owner walked in. His name was Gerry Barbero. Tony introduced him to my mother. He was looking for an Italian pastry chef. Only later did I understand what happened next. That meeting was not accidental. It was my mother's way of anchoring us in America. At the time, under Nixon-era policies, an employer could sponsor a worker for a green card if the skill set couldn't be found locally. There were formalities—a job posting in a newspaper for thirty days—but the path was clear.

My mother began working in the bakery immediately, initially under the table. Then, the paperwork followed. What I didn't understand as a child was that the visit had quietly turned into a relocation. I was enrolled in a Catholic school in Trenton—St. Joachim's—close to where we were staying. I had completed third grade in Italy and should have been placed in fourth. But I didn't speak a word of English. Because of that, they put me back in third grade.

That first day in the classroom was overwhelming. Every student spoke English. I understood nothing. I became extremely shy, deeply introverted. I felt small, invisible. That, too, became its own journey.

Reflections

This scene captures adaptation in motion.

Relocation unfolds through ordinary encounters—a shoe store, a bakery owner, a couch that becomes a bed. There is no formal declaration of immigration, only decisive action taken quietly.

The mother operates with instinct and strategic composure. Opportunity is recognized without spectacle. Stability is constructed step by step.

The classroom becomes the true threshold. Language disappears. Familiar identity dissolves. Progress resets. Immersion replaces observation.

America is no longer something seen—it becomes something lived.

Key Takeaways

1. Major life shifts are often built through small, decisive actions—not dramatic declarations.

2. Uncertainty often becomes a training ground for humility

3. New identity begins the moment old certainty disappears.

Q6

*You were adjusting to life in America—at school and at home—
without language, familiarity, or social footing.*

What was that adjustment like for you?

The adjustment to America did not last long—it lasted only
two months. During that time, there was school, and there was
home—and both felt foreign in different ways.

At school, I was extremely shy. I didn't understand much
English, and I rarely spoke in class. What made the difference
was the care the nuns showed. After regular classes, I received
private tutoring from Sister Lorenzina—a warm, gentle
woman, likely in her eighties, with gray hair and a calming
presence. She taught me English one-on-one, sitting with me
at a small bench and table tucked away in the small back room
of the classroom. That space felt safe—contained and human.

The classroom itself was more intimidating. I remember
seeing other children disciplined—slapped on their palms for
not following directions. That never happened to me, but it
added to my quietness. I stayed withdrawn, observant,

invisible—except in those moments with Sister Lorenzina, where learning felt personal rather than overwhelming.

At home, the adjustment was just as disorienting. We lived with my great-aunt and uncle, and the environment was kind, but unfamiliar. The food was different. My mother tried to preserve what felt like home—she would bring prosciutto, cheese, familiar flavors—but we had to eat them quietly in the basement. She told me we couldn't show what we were eating. I didn't understand why. I couldn't grasp why she wasn't free to express herself openly.

My great-aunt was gracious. She prepared ham, turkey—foods that were tasty, but not quite the same. That sense of concealment stayed with me: being present, but partially hidden. We visited extended family, and I was introduced to Halloween—trick-or-treating, costumes. Rituals that were distinctly American and completely unfamiliar. Everything felt vague, ungrounded, out of place. I wasn't happy.

After two months, we were called back to Italy. My brother had been hospitalized and was close to dying. I was afraid for him. At the same time, I felt unsettled in a way I could not yet explain. We had just arrived in America, and suddenly we were leaving. I did not know whether this was temporary, whether we would return, or what "home" meant anymore.

The one clear light in that experience was Sister Lorenzina.

Reflections

This scene deepens divided belonging.

School offers both intimidation and individualized care. Home offers warmth alongside concealment. Safety exists, but it is partial.

This extends into cultural disorientation. Even moments meant to be joyful—like Halloween—felt unfamiliar and ungrounded, reinforcing a quiet sense of not belonging.

Within that, Sister Lorenzina remains the one place where experience becomes steady, human, and understandable.

Sister Lorenzina becomes a fixed point within instability. The institution overwhelms; the individual steadies.

Key Takeaways

1. In unfamiliar environments, one steady relationship can anchor performance when larger systems feel overwhelming.

2. Observation and restraint are early leadership tools before voice and authority develop.

3. Identity under pressure is shaped as much by what is suppressed as by what is expressed.

Q7

When you returned to Italy, your family was facing another medical crisis.

What do you remember from that period, and how did it affect you emotionally?

For someone who generally has a strong memory, this period is strikingly absent. I don't remember much of what happened when we returned to Italy. I know that my brother was hospitalized and nearly died. Once again, a doctor made a mistake—he was given the wrong medication. I don't remember how it was resolved, only that he survived. We didn't stay long in Italy—only a couple of months—and I have no recollection of that time. Looking back, I believe I was in shock. I had just lived in America for a short period, experienced multiple displacements, and I didn't understand what was happening or why. Everything felt unstable.

When I reflect on it now, I see how that confusion shaped me internally. I became more introverted, fearful, and observant. I stayed quiet, following the movement without understanding the direction. Then we left again for America— this time with my brother. No one explained much to me. My parents shielded me from any information. In retrospect, I think my parents were trying to see whether my brother could adapt—whether he could attend school and if life in America might be viable for all of us.

When we landed at JFK Airport, Tony was waiting for us, and our arrival coincided with my ninth birthday. Tony drove us to the home of Maybelline who had four children. One was my age, one was two years older, and the other two were closer to my brother's age. They had a birthday cake for me—people gathered around, smiling, singing "Happy Birthday," trying to make me feel welcome. I didn't feel at home.

I went back to the same school and returned to Sister Lorenzina's class. I finished third grade. My mother went back to work at the bakery. My brother lived with Maybelline and her four children, attended high school, and completed his final semester. He then graduated. I stayed with my mother and her aunt. The patterns did not change much. We still hid food in the basement. I remained shy in school. The bright spot was Sister Lorenzina, who was genuinely kind and provided stability. After finishing third grade, we left again abruptly. We returned to Italy—once more uncertain about what would happen next.

Reflections

This scene introduces absence as structure.

The missing memory is not a narrative gap; it signals emotional overload.

When events exceed emotional capacity, the mind protects by softening detail. Silence becomes part of the record.

Medical error repeats. Movement repeats. Information remains withheld. Protection and confusion coexist. The child adapts without explanation.

Celebration appears—a birthday, welcoming cousins, school resumed—yet stability remains fragile. Belonging is momentary. Continuity remains elusive.

Sister Lorenzina stands as relational constancy within repeated transition. In a life defined by movement, one steady presence becomes an anchor.

The pattern becomes visible: childhood shaped more by displacement than by settlement.

Key Takeaways

1. Memory gaps may signal emotional overload; what cannot be recalled can still shape future leadership patterns.

2. Repeated instability builds adaptive capacity long before conscious understanding develops.

3. Stable relationships can anchor identity when environment and circumstance remain uncertain.

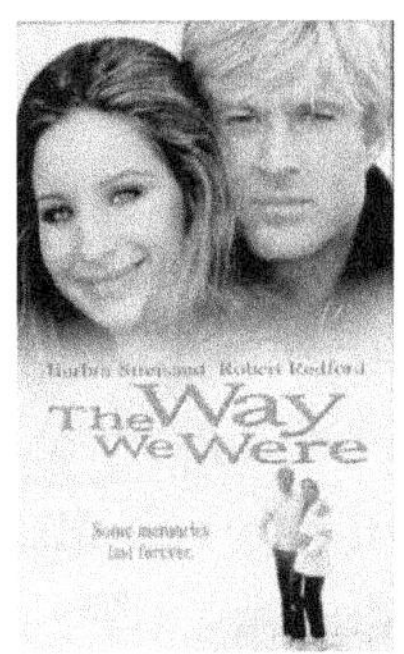

Q8

When you returned to Italy after that second stay in America, what was that experience like for you?

What I remember most upon returning to Italy is my mother's happiness. She was relieved and ecstatic because she had learned that we were going to receive permanent visas. This time, we wouldn't be visiting America. We would be moving there for good.

A few weeks later, my parents and I traveled to Naples to collect our green cards. I remember celebrating at a restaurant along the shoreline. There was a sense of arrival, of something finally opening. The bakery owner—the same man who had employed my mother—had made it possible. I don't know who paid for what. We had very little money. In fact, we had none. We were in debt. Only later did I learn the deeper context. My parents had accumulated debt, and my grandfather's second wife—my step-grandmother—had contributed significantly by writing fraudulent checks. That period involved betrayal and exploitation within the family, a long story of its own. What mattered then was that my parents saw America as a way out—a chance to start fresh.

On my mother's side, our relatives in the United States were the sisters of my grandmother and her family we met during our earlier visits. For my mother, they represented more than family; they represented possibility. My parents imagined a future where my brother might attend medical school, I was young enough to fully absorb English, and life could be rebuilt. None of this was explained to me. All I was told was: we're going back to America. This time, I knew it was permanent.

What I remember most vividly is how quickly everything ended. There was no long goodbye or closure. We packed almost overnight. A cousin drove us to the airport. We stayed near Bari and gave him a few cases of liquor from the bar—a quiet exchange that felt like a farewell. My father abandoned the café. He had leased the space. He left the keys with my godfather, who supplied the coffee for the business. The merchandise was left behind. There was no formal closure, no bankruptcy filing, no ceremony of any kind. We simply walked away. The business was gone. I never got to say my best friends—Franchino, Maurizio, Valerio—goodbye. I was deeply sad. I understood that I was leaving for good, but I didn't understand why in words—only in feeling. No one sat me down to explain. Whatever was said was likely framed as "this is better for everyone."

Only much later did I understand the truth: my parents believed this move would give us a better life. Even though they had a cash-based business and deep roots in Taranto, my mother carried a dream she had held since childhood. Coming to America had always been part of her imagination. This was her moment to claim it.

On the flight back, I remember watching a movie—The Way We Were. I didn't know then why it stayed with me, but it did. The idea that memories could last forever felt strangely personal. Years later, the song from that film became my graduating class song in grammar school. And still later, Robert Redford—one of its stars—would become a creative touchstone for me when I pursued the arts myself. At the time, I was just a child on a plane, leaving everything I knew.

But looking back, that moment quietly foreshadowed how memory, creativity, and identity would stay intertwined in my life.

Reflections

This scene reveals reinvention through sacrifice.

Departure unfolds without ceremony—no formal closing, or extended farewell. Movement replaces explanation.

A mother's relief contrasts with a child's unspoken grief. Opportunity for one generation becomes rupture for another. The abandoned café represents severance, not failure.

Even the film on the airplane becomes emotional imprint—memory, art, and identity quietly intertwining.

The later reappearance of Robert Redford reflects a subtle continuity, where early impressions return with meaning over time.

Reinvention begins before it is chosen. Growing up within unplanned, abrupt transitions introduces a quiet instability, shaping awareness, sensitivity, and an early sense of uncertainty beneath the surface.

Key Takeaways

1. Permanent change is felt emotionally before it can be explained logically.

2. Reinvention often begins before closure is complete.

3. What begins as displacement can become the foundation for future identity.

CHAPTER TWO

Graduating from Chaos

Poverty, Bullying, Domestic Violence, and the Emergence of Stability

Q9

When you returned to the United States this time, it was no longer a visit or a trial—it was a relocation.

What stands out most about those initial weeks—was there any sense of a plan?

We arrived without a real plan. The plan, if there was one, was simple: *we would figure it out*. We had the support of my American family, but stability came slowly. We stayed in one home for about a week, then moved to another. Eventually, we settled in Chambersburg, an Italian neighborhood in Trenton. That familiarity helped, but it didn't change the reality. My mother went back to work at the bakery and, through the connections she had made, my father secured a job as an auto mechanic. But, after just one week, he broke his leg. He was unable to work for six months.

On the school front, I should have been in fourth grade, but because of my Italian education—I was strong in mathematics—and despite my limited English, I skipped fourth grade entirely and was placed directly into fifth grade. I completed third grade twice—once in Italy, once in

America—and now I was advancing academically while still trying to find my footing emotionally.

My brother began his final year of high school. We were living together again, first in borrowed homes, then eventually in a small, basic apartment, on the fourth floor. I remember how often the heat didn't work. That first year was dismal. That is the word that fits. My father was unemployed. My mother became the sole provider. She worked at the bakery making Italian pastries for five dollars an hour. She also cleaned houses as a second job. We had no savings. No cushion. The church helped us with food. Everything my mother earned went toward rent and groceries.

It was poverty in its simplest form.

Reflections

This scene reveals immigration through hardship, where aspiration and endurance begin to live side by side.

Instability becomes the operating environment—moving homes, shifting schools, financial collapse. Advancement happens academically, yet emotional footing remains uneven. Progress and insecurity coexist.

The family structure reorganizes under pressure. The father is sidelined. The mother carries the economic weight. The church becomes part of the survival system.

This is no longer transition. It is sustained uncertainty. Endurance becomes normal.

Key Takeaways

1. When instability lasts, the nervous system can begin to treat uncertainty as normal.
2. Advancement without emotional security can produce hidden self-doubt.
3. Discipline often begins as survival before it becomes ambition.

Q10

In the midst of those early years marked by instability and hardship, were there moments—even small ones—that felt positive or grounding?

There were some improvements during the second year.

We moved again—this time to an apartment above an Italian deli. The owners were from Italy, and we grew close to them. That connection mattered. The apartment itself was nicer, and living directly above the deli gave us a sense of relationship and continuity. From a home perspective, life felt more grounded.

I had started making friends at school. By then, I was in sixth grade. But school was complicated. Alongside friendships, there were cliques and groups that picked on others—and I became one of the targets. The last three years of grammar school, from sixth through eighth grade, were extremely difficult. I was picked on regularly. I wasn't physically beaten, but I was pushed around, forced to eat, ridiculed, and made fun of—sometimes even by people I considered "friends." I was singled out for being foreign. My brother often had to step in to defend me.

My body had changed, too. In Italy, I had been fit and strong. In America, I gained weight, partly because of the food and because of the circumstances—I became self-conscious. Academically, I struggled. I didn't study well. I was uncomfortable, guarded, distracted. Looking back, those years were the hardest of my childhood.

At home, however, there were some signs of stabilization. Through my mother's connections and friendships, my father found a full-time job as a baker at Princeton University. That was significant. It came with benefits—including a program that allowed children of low-income employees to attend college with little to no tuition. At the time, we were excited by that possibility. My brother's path diverged. He graduated high school but didn't want to go to college. Instead, he began working as a security officer, trying to find his direction.

The following year, we moved again—back to my great-aunt's home. The second-floor apartment above her house became available, and we took it. It was a step forward. My brother and I had our own bedroom in the attic. We lived there for two years. That move brought its own dynamics—and its own challenges.

Reflections

This scene carries tension that continues to shape the experience.

Housing improves and financial stability begins to return. At the same time, social pressure intensifies. Home offers grounding while school remains a place of exposure.

Belonging proves to be layered. Grounding in one environment can coexist with exposure in another.

The bullying is steady. It accumulates. Repetition shapes identity more than single events.

The father's role strengthens again through meaningful work at Princeton. The presence of the university introduces a new horizon for the family. Possibility enters the environment, quietly shaping how the future is imagined.

Growth here takes the form of endurance under constant visibility.

Key Takeaways

1. Environmental stability does not guarantee social belonging.

2. Repeated social pressure shapes identity more powerfully than isolated conflict.

3. Proximity to opportunity can influence ambition long before access becomes real.

Q11

You've described that living upstairs at your great-aunt's house brought more physical stability—more space, privacy, and continuity—but also a new set of challenges.

What were those challenges?

The last two years of grammar school—seventh and eighth grade—were the most difficult period of my childhood.

I was eleven years old, and life felt chaotic. There were elements of improvement alongside deep instability. We were living in a better home which brought more space and physical comfort. My English continued to improve. I joined a soccer team, and playing again—especially on Sundays— reminded me of who I had been before everything became complicated. Those moments were genuinely happy.

But school remained painful. I continued to be picked on. The social pressure never fully lifted. The most sensitive and confusing part of that period involved distant cousins close to my age. I don't remember exactly when it began. I remember only that what happened was neither violent nor forced, yet it was not understood. It occurred a few times, one at a time, and

I moved through it without language or clarity for what was taking place. I didn't tell anyone. I simply accepted it.

At the time, I don't recall crying or reacting outwardly. I was simply navigating what unfolded, going along as I understood life then. Looking back now, it feels like watching a film of a boy with no one to speak to, no framework to interpret what he was experiencing, and no guidance to help him process it.

From this distance, I feel deep compassion for that boy. If I was watching his movie, I would be in tears.

Reflections

This scene unfolds through silence.

Stability increases externally—better housing, improved language, moments of joy through soccer—yet internally, confusion deepens. Growth and vulnerability coexist.

The experiences with distant cousins are described without accusation or embellishment. What stands out is absence of guidance.

There was no language, framework, or adult conversation to interpret what was happening.

The child adapts the only way he knows how: by continuing forward.

From this distance, compassion becomes the corrective lens.

What once felt confusing is now understood as a moment that lacked protection.

Key Takeaways

1. When guidance is absent, children are left to make sense of situations on their own.

2. Emotional restraint often begins as a form of protection.

3. Compassion toward younger selves strengthens discernment in adulthood.

Q12

Those years sound like a very difficult time in your life. How did that period begin to shape what came next for you?

Things did not get better immediately. In many ways, they got worse.

Domestic violence entered our home. My parents began arguing intensely. I don't remember what triggered the fights—only the escalation. My father became physically abusive toward my mother. She fought back verbally, emotionally, sometimes physically. It was chaotic.

My brother was often not around. When he was, he tended to leave. I became the one in the middle. I remember separating them—an eleven-year-old boy stepping between two adults. I remember comforting my mother afterward. She had bruises on her arms. She was slapped, hit. There were no dramatic scenes afterward. No police, no conversations no explanations. After the fights, my father would leave. I would stay with my mother comforting her until she fell asleep. And then life would continue as if nothing had happened. It was never discussed, explained, or acknowledged. I remember one moment when my father asked for forgiveness, but no one ever spoke to me about what I had seen or done. This went on for three or four years. During that time, I also began carrying responsibilities beyond my age—cleaning the house, doing local grocery shopping, preparing simple meals when my parents were exhausted or in conflict. I was eleven or twelve, but I moved through the house as if I were older.

At the same time, my brother was working security jobs and struggling with expectations to go to college. My parents were in conflict over his future. I was finishing grammar school while being bullied regularly. My father worked two jobs—at Princeton University as a baker and at Educational Testing Service as a cleaner. My mother continued working long hours at the bakery and cleaning homes afterwards. I tried to find small places to breathe by creating small performances at home—dressing up, inventing characters, putting on shows for myself and sometimes for others. It was another way to redirect energy, to create light where there was tension. I played football with friends. I joined Little League baseball— I wasn't very good, but I showed up. My life was tightly controlled. I had to be home at a strict time. My friends made fun of me for it. I continued to be ridiculed for existing.

Then something shifted. One morning, my mother noticed a house for sale on the same street as the bakery—only a few minutes away. For the first time in a long while, there was good news. That house became a turning point. Things began to improve once we found it.

Reflections

This scene marks the moment when responsibility enters the child's life.

Mediation, protection, and silence become daily responsibilities.

What stands out is the absence of processing. There are no explanations, no structured repair. Life resumes. The weight remains.

Alongside chaos, small forms of structure emerge—sports, strict schedules, creative expression. These activities provide small forms of containment and breathing room.

Responsibility arrives early. Endurance becomes habit.

Presence begins forming under pressure.

Key Takeaways

1. Leadership often begins when we step into responsibility before anyone formally asks us to.

2. Structure and discipline often begin as survival tools and gradually grow into strengths.

3. The ability to stay present under pressure is built through repeated exposure to instability.

Q13

What changed for you once your family moved into that home—and how did that change begin to shape who you were becoming?

My parents buying that house was a major turning point for our family.

I remember the first moment I walked into it clearly. It was a semi-attached home in a very good neighborhood, just half a block from where my mother worked. Three bedrooms. A bathroom upstairs. A backyard. Old furniture, but solid bones. The woman selling the house connected deeply with my mother. She said my mom reminded her of her own mother— Italian, hardworking, resilient. The house cost around thirty thousand dollars. She held the mortgage herself. The payments were manageable—three to four hundred dollars a month. The paperwork was simple. The opportunity felt human and my mother was ecstatic.

At first, it felt like something had finally stabilized. My father was still working in Princeton, but tensions followed us into the new home. He became jealous of my mother's work at the Italian bakery, resentful that she was thriving while he felt diminished. Eventually, he quit both Princeton University and Educational Testing Service. That decision erased my chance to attend college tuition-free—something that had once felt like a lifeline. He went to work at the same bakery as my mom, baking bread. My mother earned slightly more than he did. The imbalance fed resentment. Arguments continued. The abuse at home did not stop. But for me, something else shifted.

After graduating grammar school, I entered high school—a Catholic school nearby. It was a completely different environment. No bullying. No targeting. Even students who had once bullied me became friends. It felt like a reset. Every year, I did better. Academically, I thrived. Mathematics, physics, chemistry—I earned almost all A's. I played soccer on the junior varsity team. I didn't have girlfriends. I was still shy. But I was respected. Liked. Seen. I graduated ranked twenty-fifth in my class. Two major turning points came during my final year.

One involved my body. Old stitches from my childhood surgery in Italy began emerging from my abdomen. I was taken to the University of Pennsylvania hospital, where a surgeon reopened the original incision and removed remnants left behind years earlier. He asked me whether the doctor who operated on me in Italy had been licensed—God only knows what he found inside. The doctor did not go into details. He treated me largely as a charity case, charging just enough for insurance to cover it. I spent five days recovering in the hospital.

The other turning point was way overdue. By then, I was taller than my father—over six feet. One night, during an argument between my parents, something in me shifted. I stepped between them again, but this time I did not step back. I pinned him against the wall and told him calmly that if he ever touched my mother again, I would not allow it. It was not rage—it was resolve.

In earlier confrontations between my parents, I had lifted tables, sending plates flying—not to cause harm, but to interrupt the chaos. That night was different. A boundary had finally been set. After that confrontation, the physical abuse stopped. The verbal tension did not disappear, but something fundamental had changed. A line had been drawn—no more physical abuse.

When I graduated high school, the feeling was different. It was celebratory. My brother graduated from the Trenton Police Academy at the same time. For the first time, there was a sense of forward movement and emergence.

Reflections

This scene unfolds through a series of turning points.

Stability begins with the house. For the first time in years, the family has a place that feels rooted. The environment changes, even as tensions inside the home continue to surface.

At school, a different shift begins. High school brings a new social environment where respect replaces ridicule. Academic strength returns, friendships form, and confidence gradually rebuilds. Structure in learning and recognition among peers begin reshaping identity.

The surgery at the University of Pennsylvania closes a lingering physical chapter from childhood. A wound that began years earlier is finally addressed, reinforcing the sense that the past no longer controls the present.

With these shifts building quietly, the confrontation with the father becomes the decisive moment. Protection becomes conscious leadership. A boundary is established calmly and clearly.

Key Takeaways

1. Stability creates the foundation from which confidence and direction can begin to grow.

2. Leadership requires the courage to establish boundaries when protection becomes necessary.

3. Endurance evolves into agency as competence, confidence, and clarity begin to align.

CHAPTER THREE
Choosing to Finish

Momentum, Grief, and Earned Completion

# Q14

With stability finally taking root after years of disruption, how did you step into the next phase of your life?

Looking back, the years that followed became the best period our family ever experienced together.

My parents were both working at the bakery. My mother was highly respected—known as one of the top bakers. She still earned low wages, seven or eight dollars an hour, but for a woman in that role at the time, her standing mattered. She carried herself with pride. People trusted her. My father was different. Although the domestic violence had ended, his anger and frustration remained. He struggled at work. He didn't take care of himself. He smoked heavily—nearly a pack a day—and had high blood pressure. Still, the relationship between my parents had softened. It was smoother and calmer.

And as a family, something beautiful emerged. Every summer, my parents were able to take three weeks of paid vacation. We rented a house at the Jersey Shore. For three weeks, life slowed down. We lived by the rhythm of the beach. After the surgery and the long period of recovery that followed, being able to swim in the ocean again felt liberating. For the first time in years, my body felt free in the water. My father would come out for a few hours, then return home to cook. My mother stayed on the beach all day with me. My brother spent time there, then went out at night. I didn't have a girlfriend. I walked the boardwalk in the evenings, observing, taking everything in. Watching life. Those summers were the best times of our lives.

Academically, I graduated high school strong, but standardized testing didn't reflect that. I took the SAT twice and scored in the average range, despite my strength in math. Instead of applying to a four-year university, I enrolled at Mercer County Community College, which at the time was highly regarded. I stayed there three years instead of two, taking extra courses. I took the placement exam and aced it. Faculty questioned why I was there, given my abilities. But I knew the answer, even if I couldn't articulate it fully at the time. I wanted to stay close to home. After a childhood defined by movement, instability, and separation, proximity felt like safety.

Around that time, I also began finding rhythm outside of academics. I spent long stretches walking alone in nature—through the parks near the college, along quiet paths, sometimes without destination. I swam regularly. I paid attention to my body in a way I never had before. Silence, movement, and physical care became grounding forces. I didn't think of it as anything philosophical then—it was instinctive. But it helped me regulate myself, listen inwardly, and create space where something creative could eventually emerge. Community college turned out to be a gift. That's where things truly opened up for me—intellectually, socially, and internally. During that time, I started dating. Over the summer, I met someone from Canada, a few years younger than me. We connected. She invited me to her prom in Montreal. After graduating from community college, I took an overnight train there. It was one of my first experiences of choosing connection rather than reacting to circumstance. For the first time, life wasn't just happening to me. I was stepping into it.

Reflections

This scene introduces rhythm after years of volatility.

The summers at the shore establish cadence—time unfolding without rupture. Togetherness exists in ordinary moments: beach routines, evening walks, shared space without escalation. Stability is felt in the body before it is interpreted in language.

The decision to attend community college marks a subtle but defining shift. Proximity becomes intentional. After years of imposed movement, remaining close to home becomes a form of agency.

Nature enters as formative ground. Walking, swimming, silence, and solitude begin shaping the internal landscape in conscious ways. Regulation strengthens. Awareness deepens. The body and environment start working together rather than in tension.

Participation begins replacing reaction.

Direction forms quietly.

Adulthood begins here as grounded expansion.

Key Takeaways

1. Real stability gives you room to choose—but growth begins when you decide deliberately, not by default.

2. The environments you choose—where you live, who you stay near, how you care for your body—shape your long-term direction.

3. True expansion begins when you move toward something, not just away from something.

Q15

Your years at community college marked a significant period of growth.

How did that experience shape your development during that time?

Those years became a turning point in every way. For the first time, I felt fully at peace in an academic environment. The college was twenty minutes from home. I had a routine. I brought my own lunch—leftovers or a sandwich my mother prepared. I swam regularly, three times a week. Sundays were for soccer.

Academically, I thrived. I was a mathematics major and took the most advanced courses available—advanced calculus, integration, and higher-level mathematics. I completed two full years of university physics using the same textbook by Halliday & Resnick taught at Princeton University. That mattered deeply to me. Even though I hadn't gone to Princeton, I was studying from the same material. I earned all A's except for one B in English and graduated magna cum laude. I received multiple awards and scholarships— including a one-thousand-dollar scholarship for the highest grade point average. I earned recognition in mathematics, physics, and Spanish. Some of my advanced calculus exams were archived and shared with future students as examples of how to perform on exams.

What truly shaped me during those years was my love for solving problems. The Halliday and Resnick physics textbook became almost like a companion to me. I worked through nearly every exercise in the book, sometimes staying up late into the night just to see the next problem through to its solution. My father would wake at three in the morning to leave for work, and I would still be at the table, pencil in hand, immersed in equations. I loved the clarity of it. A problem appeared complex at first, yet with patience and discipline it could be understood and resolved. That experience stayed with me. It quietly shaped how I would later approach challenges in life and work.

My parents attended my graduation. They were in tears. Life had rhythm, extending beyond school. Home life reflected a rare period of stability. My parents were doing better. My father even stopped smoking for a period. Summers continued—vacations together, time away, a sense of normalcy. My brother was thriving as well. He excelled at the police academy and became engaged to an Italian woman whose parents, from Sicily, owned a pizzeria. The families grew close. I dated her older sister briefly for a few months but the connection felt easy, familiar, and connected. I was still inexperienced, yet I was beginning to understand connection—being present, participating, and choosing engagement rather than simply observing life from a distance.

From a family perspective, those last few years were the best of our lives. I felt grounded, supported and capable.

I didn't yet know that it wouldn't last long.

Reflections

This scene consolidates earned stability.

Academic excellence reflects alignment rather than compensation. Structure meets capacity, and performance follows naturally.

Studying from the same Princeton textbooks represents quiet resolution. Access shifts form, yet mastery remains real. Comparison dissolves.

Domestic steadiness supports intellectual expansion. Stability becomes lived experience rather than temporary relief.

Routine—swimming, soccer, proximity, rhythm—demonstrates self-regulation becoming internal. Discipline is no longer reactive. It is integrated.

This period stands complete in itself—grounded, capable, and whole.

Key Takeaways

1. Sustained performance emerges when ability is supported by stable conditions.

2. Routine, proximity, and physical discipline form strategic foundations for long-term growth.

3. Confidence becomes durable when demonstrated mastery aligns with respected benchmarks.

Q16

*After a period of stability and forward momentum, what shifted
that sent your life in a different direction?*

After graduating from community college the momentum
continued—at least for a while.

I applied to several universities—Rutgers, the University of
Pennsylvania, and Penn State. University of Pennsylvania held
symbolic meaning for me, connected to the surgeon who had
once intervened in my life. Penn State appealed through
football and culture. But both were out-of-state, and the
tuition would have been significantly higher. Rutgers, as a
state university, made practical sense. I had received a one-
thousand-dollar scholarship. Room and board cost
approximately twenty-five hundred dollars per year. I
qualified for a student loan, which made enrollment possible.

I enrolled at Rutgers University in New Brunswick, majoring
in mathematics with a Bachelor of Arts, a minor in economics,
and a sub-minor in Spanish. It was a balanced curriculum—
analytical, economic, linguistic. For the first time, I would be

living on campus, about thirty minutes from home. At first, I liked being alone and finally away from home. But I wasn't prepared for dormitory life—shared spaces, constant stimulation, unfamiliar rhythms. Around that time, I had my first sexual experience—a one-night encounter that felt more like a rite of passage than a meaningful connection.

During the week, I stayed on campus. On weekends, I returned home. That's where the imbalance began. It wasn't the return of old chaos—the family was still functioning—but something subtler surfaced. For the first time, I was stepping into independence, and my absence altered the emotional field at home. My mother was deeply loving—yet intensely attached. When I came back on weekends, her excitement to see me translated into closeness that felt overwhelming. I felt myself pulled back into familiar roles, familiar gravity. I didn't yet know how to hold independence without feeling disloyal—or autonomy without carrying guilt. Within two months, my body collapsed under the strain. I was exhausted, depressed, and unmotivated. I took only one or two exams and did poorly. I stopped going to class. I returned home and stayed there.

At the end of December, I received a letter from Dean's Office at Rutgers informing me that I was facing expulsion due to non-attendance. That letter changed everything. I wrote a three-page appeal immediately. I explained my family situation, the emotional weight I was carrying, the internal conflict I hadn't yet learned how to navigate. I didn't know if they would accept it to allow me to return.

It was a wake-up call—not about intelligence or ability, but about something deeper I had not yet resolved.

Reflections

This scene reveals the gap between external momentum and inner separation.

External progress continues—admission to Rutgers, financial support, independence—but emotional separation from home has not yet matured. Structure shifts quickly. Identity lags behind.

The oscillation between campus and home reveals the tension. Autonomy during the week. Emotional gravity on weekends. The strain builds quietly.

The Rutgers letter becomes a moment of clarity. For the first time, consequences make visible what internal imbalance had already begun.

Capability remained intact. What was missing was emotional independence.

This moment exposes the difference between achievement and self-possession.

Key Takeaways

1. True independence grows from emotional separation as well as physical distance.

2. Achievement is sustainable only when inner alignment supports it.

3. Consequences can serve as clarifying feedback when imbalance goes unaddressed.

Q17

Receiving a termination letter from Rutgers must have been jarring—especially after years of academic excellence and momentum.

What was the outcome of your appeal?

After submitting my appeal to Rutgers, I entered a period of waiting—and uncertainty. I had stayed up all night writing that letter. I cared deeply. I did not know whether they would take me back.

At home, the weight of everything caught up with me. I was exhausted and depressed. My mother, seeing it, asked my father to speak with me. Life at home had improved. He had been proud of me. He had stood in tears at my graduation. Yet he was still carrying his own internal battles—health concerns, work frustrations, emotions he did not easily express. I knew that side of him too.

When he came to speak with me, I braced myself. Instead, something unexpected happened. He was calm. He told me not to worry. That if I needed time, I could take time. That something would work out. There was no pressure. Only steadiness. That moment mattered. I realized something essential about myself. Much of my life had unfolded in environments filled with tension and chaos, and I had often stepped in to organize, stabilize, and resolve what was around me. Yet in that moment I saw the other side of it as well: when there is harmony and steadiness, I expand and perform at my best.

A week later, Rutgers accepted my appeal. The condition was clear: I had to make up the four classes I had abandoned in the fall while carrying a full spring load. I agreed. I arranged independent study for the four previous courses and enrolled in four new ones—eight classes total. By then, I had ended my relationship with my Italian girlfriend. There was no emotional pull back home. I stayed on campus. My parents visited once a month, but I did not return home on weekends. I focused completely. That semester, I excelled. I earned nearly all A's. I rediscovered my love of studying—the same joy I had felt at community college.

At Rutgers, the library became my haven. I wasn't seeking closeness or belonging. I knew many people, but I wasn't deeply connected to anyone. I was building something inside myself. I stayed on campus during the summer and took two courses—one in mathematics and one in Italian. I had never formally studied advanced Italian grammar; I had left school in Italy after third grade. That summer filled a quiet gap. During those weeks, I met another mathematics major. She became my first long-term girlfriend, and we were together for over a year. That summer also marked what would be the final memories as a family. We traveled together—to Montreal and then back to Atlantic City, NJ. It was a joyful, best, and only vacation outside of the US—unknowingly it would be our last together.

I returned to Rutgers for my senior year and earned all A's again in the fall semester. On New Year's Eve, my parents, my girlfriend, and I celebrated at a restaurant. I didn't yet know that another dramatic event was waiting just weeks ahead.

Reflections

This scene restores continuity after rupture.

The appeal is accepted, but the deeper shift occurs at home. Kindness replaces confrontation. Emotional steadiness supports recovery.

Academic excellence returns once internal balance stabilizes. Structure provides direction; harmony sustains performance.

The decision to remain on campus marks differentiation. Distance becomes intentional.

Identity strengthens through deliberate choice. Momentum resumes—grounded, disciplined, and internally aligned.

Key Takeaways

1. Performance expands in environments of harmony, while leadership often emerges when chaos calls for order and resolution.

2. True resilience includes knowing when to create distance from unresolved dynamics in order to grow.

3. Sustainable excellence emerges when discipline is paired with calm, not fear.

Q18

You entered the new year with momentum restored—academically strong and emotionally steadier.

Then what happened next?

I began the year in a good place. My family felt strong. My brother was thriving in the police force and on track to become a detective. My mother and father were working. There was stability. The only shadow was my father's health—high blood pressure, heavy smoking. A doctor had warned him directly to stop smoking, even sketching a symbol of death on a piece of paper as a warning. A few days later, the warning became reality.

On a Saturday morning, in late January, I was at school when my brother called. My father had been rushed to the hospital. I drove home immediately, frantic, and bumped into another car on the highway. No damage—but it spoke to my state of mind. When I arrived home, there was blood on the living room carpet. My father's blood. At the hospital, my father was in a coma. He had suffered an aneurysm. He had still been breathing when the ambulance arrived, but at some point in the hospital, he slipped fully into unconsciousness. He was placed on a respirator. Doctors told us there was no hope—that he would remain in a vegetative state. I loved my father deeply. My relationship with him was different from what outsiders might assume. We shared openly. He shared stories about his life. I never held the abuse against him. It was never spoken, processed, or named. To me, I was losing my best friend because despite how he acted at times, I recognized his heart was broken a long time ago by his upbringing. I loved him and I understood parts of his pain.

My father had grown up in hardship of his own. He lost his mother when he was still a boy—she died at only thirty years old. His father was often absent and unfaithful, and much of his upbringing fell to others. Some of those years were unstable and left their own scars. Yet despite everything he carried, he had a generous heart. One small memory stayed with me. He used to hang his flour-covered work jeans on a hook inside the basement door after returning from the bakery. In the pocket were folded bills—usually twenty-dollar notes. He shared with me more than once, "If you ever need money, just take it." I rarely did. Just knowing it was there, and that he trusted me that way, meant everything. It was his quiet way of showing love.

For ten days, he remained in a coma. I visited him daily. I spoke to him about soccer games, about life, about what was happening. Before the coma deepened completely, there was a moment I will never forget: he squeezed our hands. Tears ran from his closed eyes. He was saying goodbye. Then he never woke up again. I often wonder what happened in those moments—whether the ambulance or the hospital failed him. That thought never left me. It became part of me. A vigilance around health, care, and oversight that later defined how I looked after my mother—and how I manage everything in my life.

On February 10th, we made the decision to remove life support. I was the most composed among us—not because I felt less, but because I knew my father would never have wanted to live that way. Thirty seconds after the respirator was disconnected, he passed. I watched my father die. I collapsed. I cried on the hospital floor for hours. For days, grief consumed me. In the days that followed, reality set in quickly. My father had canceled his life insurance shortly before he passed. There was very little money. My mother and brother were working, but we were not financially secure.

Without fully thinking it through, I stepped forward. I arranged for my father to be placed in a mausoleum at St. Francis—a Catholic site connected to my high school community. I secured a space not only for him, but for my mother as well. I also arranged for a bench to be installed near the fountain beneath the statue of St. Francis, engraved in his memory with a message from our family. I was still a student. I had no income. I placed a small deposit and promised to pay the balance over time. Because they knew me—because they had watched me grow—they trusted my word. I paid it off years later, after I began working. In that moment, something shifted. I was no longer simply the son. I had become the one making family decisions.

The funeral was overwhelming. Because of my brother's standing in the police department, my father received a police funeral. Officers stood guard at the wake. We were escorted by police cars to the service. The captain of the Trenton Police Department attended. My brother was promoted to detective around the same time. It was all happening at once—loss and recognition, death and advancement.

At Rutgers, the response was extraordinary. The dean encouraged me to withdraw from the semester—without penalty—and return in the fall, graduating in December instead of May. They told me plainly: *this time, take care of yourself.* I still get emotional thinking about that kindness. I went away alone that weekend to my girlfriend's family beach house to reflect on my next steps. I brought my books. I needed *silence* to choose whether to continue or to pause. My mother and brother couldn't understand why I left. They thought I was running away. But I was doing what I had learned to do my entire life: I was reflecting in silence— playing out the various scenarios in my mind, like watching different scene options for a movie.

Reflections

This scene marks the emergence of stewardship.

Grief is immediate, yet responsibility activates without hesitation. Financial uncertainty is present, yet action moves forward.

The mausoleum arrangement reflects quiet authority. Trust is extended based on character rather than capital. Leadership emerges through decisive action.

Institutional compassion and personal vigilance intersect. Loss deepens awareness. Awareness strengthens discernment.

Solitude at the beach house becomes a moment of calibration. The father's voice shifts from external presence to internal compass. Guidance becomes integrated.

Identity reorganizes under pressure. The son becomes the decision-maker. Compassion also deepens. The ability to see the humanity within flawed people becomes part of leadership itself.

Key Takeaways

1. Leadership matures when responsibility is assumed before resources are secured.

2. Dignity in moments of loss defines character more than achievement in moments of gain.

3. In moments of grief, creating space for reflection strengthens clarity and prepares the ground for future decisions.

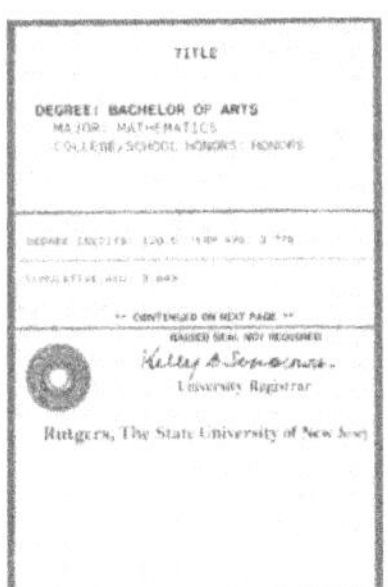

Q19

What did you do during those days away—emotionally and internally—as you faced the decision ahead, and how did you arrive at clarity about your path forward?

I remember that weekend with absolute clarity. I went alone to a small beach house. It was silent with no television or radio. Just me, my thoughts, and books—which I never opened. I cooked one of my father's favorite Italian dishes— ragu with sausage over orecchiette pasta. I prepared the sauce slowly, cooked the pasta and sausage, and poured myself a glass of wine. I stayed from Friday night through Sunday. I walked along the beach, reflecting on one question over and over: What would my father want me to do if he were here today?

I felt his presence and heard his voice. The answer came without struggle. He would want me to go back and finish with honors. By the time I returned home, I was at peace. The decision had been made. I returned to Rutgers. My roommates, professors, and the dean were surprised. I stayed

on campus and focused entirely on my work. That semester—
the most difficult of my academic career—became my
strongest. I didn't party. I didn't distract myself. I studied. I
grieved. I lived in solitude. I remember listening to *Love Don't
Live Here Anymore*—the Madonna remake—and crying while
I studied. Those tears did not weaken me. They were part of
the process. I attended a few campus gatherings. I spoke only
occasionally by phone with my girlfriend attending Wheaton.
The distance allowed me to stay focused.

Graduation mattered more than anything else. And I finished.
I graduated magna cum laude. During graduation week, I
stayed on campus, celebrated, and allowed myself to enjoy
what I had earned. On graduation day, my mother and my
brother were there—proud and present. My girlfriend was
there, as was my brother's fiancée. It was a beautiful day. I
missed my father deeply. The feeling was bittersweet—
celebratory and melancholic at the same time. But I knew,
without question, that he would have been proud. He had seen
me graduate from community college. He had witnessed that
milestone. This one, I did for him. He was the force behind my
decision.

And I finished.

Reflections

This scene centers on stillness.

Solitude is chosen. Grief is carried alongside decision. Silence
becomes a space for clear deliberation.

The father's voice moves from memory into an internal compass. Guidance lives within. Direction now arises from inner alignment.

The semester that follows demonstrates coherence under strain. Focus and sorrow coexist. Completion becomes an expression of alignment.

The repetition at the end—*And I finished.*—lands with earned simplicity. The emotional journey continues, while direction stands clear.

Key Takeaways

1. Stillness allows values to clarify direction when emotion is intense.

2. Discipline is most durable when it includes, rather than excludes, grief.

3. Completion under pressure strengthens identity more than success under ease.

CHAPTER FOUR

Acceleration Without Alignment

External Mastery, Relentless Momentum,

and the Cost of Imbalance

Q20

After graduating from Rutgers, you reached a significant milestone—achieved in the shadow of loss after your father's passing. What was the period immediately after graduation like for you?

After graduating from Rutgers, I was exhausted—deeply exhausted—and also relieved.

At the same time, I was in pain. I had been operating at an extremely high pace for a long time, pushing myself relentlessly to finish what I had started. Once it was done, my body completely collapsed.

For the first month, I slowed down, rested, and I watched TV. One thing I became almost obsessed with during that period was the Iran-Contra affair, which was being televised extensively at the time. Watching it unfold awakened something in me. It made me realize that I wanted to apply my talents—especially my background in mathematics and analytical thinking—to work that mattered, to systems that had real-world impact.

That curiosity led me to explore several paths. I considered the Navy and spent a weekend in Groton, Connecticut, learning about the five-year Navy officer's program. The education and training were prestigious, but the idea of being confined in a submarine for six months did not feel aligned with who I was. I also explored the FBI. They were genuinely interested in my profile—my academic performance, mathematics background, and fluency in Spanish and Italian. The only limitation was that I needed five years of professional work experience. They encouraged me to return once I had that experience, leaving that door open for the future.

Ultimately, through a family friend, I was introduced to a senior vice president at New Jersey National Bank—known today as Wells Fargo. The bank had just launched a comprehensive executive management program, one of the first of its kind. I interviewed and was accepted. I began the program in the first week of January with a salary of seventeen thousand dollars a year, which was modest given my education. But I saw the opportunity clearly. The program offered exposure to every part of banking—operations, finance, leadership, and systems.

In hindsight, that decision became foundational. It quietly paved the way for my entire professional career.

Reflections

This scene marks a shift from recovery to orientation.

The televised Iran-Contra hearings widen the lens—systems, accountability, consequence.

Exhaustion surfaces immediately after completion, signaling that performance had been sustained through force rather than balance. The collapse is accumulated strain finally acknowledged.

What follows is intentional exploration. Military service, federal investigation, and banking each represent different expressions of structure and impact.

Some paths required additional time. Others required internal alignment. The evaluation is thoughtful rather than impulsive.

The decision to enter banking is pragmatic on the surface and strategic underneath. Exposure across functions replaces narrow specialization.

This moment refines ambition. Direction becomes deliberate.

Key Takeaways

1. Periods of collapse after achievement often contain the clearest signals about what alignment truly requires.

2. Precision in thinking naturally seeks systems where accuracy, accountability, and consequence matter.

3. Choosing environments for exposure and learning over title or pay compounds into long-term leadership strength.

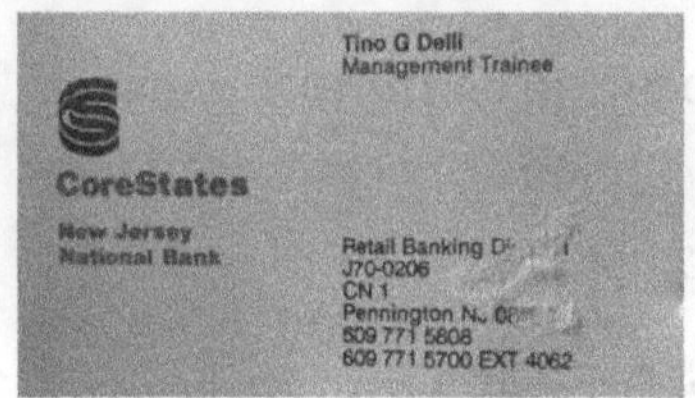

Q21

You entered the professional world through a comprehensive management program at a major bank.

What was that experience like, and how did it begin shaping your skills and direction?

The program was comprehensive by design. I rotated through every part of the banking system: teller operations, customer service, internal controls, analytics, branch management, commercial lending, and client relationships. I learned how money actually moved—risk evaluation, employee training and management, and the development of trust between the bank and the businesses it served. The work suited me. My background in mathematics made financial analysis feel intuitive, and I quickly became comfortable working directly with clients—including small business owners—discussing numbers, strategy, and lending decisions. I wasn't just analyzing systems; I was analyzing numbers and engaging with a variety of people.

By the end of the program, I had emerged as the top graduate among seven trainees. Graduates were typically placed into assistant branch manager or junior corporate roles. Instead, I was offered a role in the small business banking division, managing a ten-million-dollar lending portfolio. I received a modest raise and a clear signal that the organization saw long-term potential in me.

At the same time, another opportunity began to surface. My cousin—a retired Air Force colonel and gifted engineer—and I spent hours together solving mathematics and physics problems, often scribbling equations on napkins. He was working with Science Applications International Corporation on defense contracts connected to Raytheon and Lockheed, supporting systems used during the Gulf War, including the Patriot missile program. Through him, I interviewed for an entry-level staff scientist position focused on mathematical modeling of electronic defense systems. The role would be based in New Hampshire, just outside Boston, and it came with a starting annual salary of twenty-nine thousand dollars—significantly higher than what I was earning at the bank.

When I informed the bank, I was asked to meet with a senior vice president, Jack Neary, a respected leader within the organization. He was candid. They had invested heavily in me. They believed I had what it took to rise all the way to the top— even using the word "president." To keep me, they offered to match the salary—about a fifty percent increase. I took a few days to reflect. In the end, I chose the scientist role. It wasn't a rejection of banking. It was an evolution. Banking had refined me—it had taught me rigor, discipline, executive presence, and how complex systems function. Moving into a scientific and engineering environment felt like a step forward, not sideways. I was bringing precision, polish, and leadership into a world that was technically brilliant but often operationally unrefined. I trusted that combination would matter.

This scene marks the first fully conscious professional pivot.

The banking program provides structural literacy. Institutions reveal their internal mechanics—risk evaluation, decision frameworks, and the operational foundations of trust.

Systems thinking and human consequence become visible together. Just as important, the role required learning to read people.

Lending decisions were never only numerical; they involved understanding character, judgment, and credibility. Analytical skill began integrating with human insight.

Recognition arrives clearly: top graduate, expanded responsibility, leadership potential.

The decision process remains centered on trajectory rather than praise.

The transition into scientific modeling expands the leadership operating range.

Financial systems thinking meets technical precision. Analytical depth extends beyond commerce into engineered systems.

Competencies begin to layer. The career starts to take architectural form.

Key Takeaways

1. Early career choices that prioritize exposure to systems over titles create long-term leverage.

2. Technical analysis becomes far more powerful when paired with the ability to read people and understand human judgment.

3. Leadership depth grows through the integration of analytical rigor, human judgment, and disciplined execution across domains.

Q22

Leaving banking for a staff scientist role required relocation and greater responsibility for your family.

What was that transition like as you moved to New Hampshire and stepped into highly sensitive technical work?

After my father passed away, I effectively became the head of the family. My mother stopped working. She returned to the bakery briefly, but emotionally she couldn't sustain it. At that point, I was supporting her financially while still working at the bank—and in the evenings, I was also working part-time as a restaurant host and manager. I was carrying two jobs, holding the family together. My brother married very quickly after my father's death. I didn't want to leave my mother alone.

When I accepted the scientist position, I made the decision to bring her with me. At the time, I was also in a relationship, and together we relocated to New Hampshire. We initially stayed with my cousin and his wife in Nashua for a few weeks, and then we found our own condo in Merrimack, New Hampshire. The move turned out to be good for my mother—though I didn't fully understand how fragile she was at the time.

Years later, she shared something with me that has stayed with me ever since. There was a train track behind our brand-new condo, and during that period she was deeply depressed. She shared with me that she had considered walking onto the tracks to end her life. One morning, she was about to leave and head for the tracks until she heard me calling her. In that moment, she realized I needed her—and that knowledge stopped her. I've carried that with me ever since. Without realizing it consciously at the time, I had become the protector of the family, especially of my mother. That role—of responsibility, vigilance, and care—continued to shape who I was becoming.

Professionally, the work in New Hampshire was exceptional. I co-authored three classified scientific documents under U.S. government secret clearance. The work involved mathematical analysis and nuclear assessment of electronic systems used in the Patriot missile system—technology that would later be deployed during the Gulf War. It was prestigious, deeply technical, and intellectually fulfilling. For the first time, I was fully expressing my scientific background at a high level. The position lasted only about a year. When the government contract expired, the work concluded. I searched for additional opportunities in the area, but at the same time, a contact back in New Jersey reached out. They were looking for a restaurant manager.

Once again, life pivoted. We returned to New Jersey, to the home we already had, and I took on the role of managing a large, seafood, and lobster restaurant in Princeton, earning thirty-five thousand dollars a year. That decision brought us back home after a one-year chapter that had been both profound and formative.

This scene deepens the pattern of responsibility that has been forming throughout the narrative.

Family stability shifts again, and responsibility moves forward naturally.

Financial provision, relocation, and emotional steadiness converge quietly.

The disclosure from his mother, shared years later, reframes that period.

What appeared externally as relocation and professional advancement also carried unseen emotional fragility.

Protection now flows in both directions—first from parent to child, and now from child to parent.

Professionally, the contrast is notable. Highly classified technical work requiring precision, discipline, and discretion unfolds alongside domestic vulnerability and grief.

The coexistence of these environments reinforces an emerging capacity: composure across extremes.

The return to New Jersey continues an established rhythm in the narrative—pivot without collapse, transition without identity loss. Skills transfer.

Dignity remains intact. Direction adjusts. Responsibility is no longer circumstantial. It is becoming structural.

Key Takeaways

1. Leadership often begins as responsibility assumed quietly, before it is ever recognized publicly.

2. The ability to integrate technical rigor with human care creates uncommon resilience and credibility.

3. Strategic pivots grounded in relationships and values compound more reliably than rigid career plans.

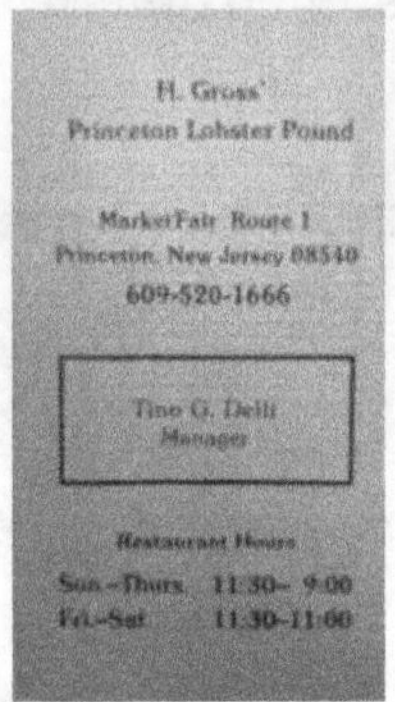

Q23

After leaving a technical scientific role near Boston, you stepped into managing a large restaurant in Princeton.

What was that transition like for you?

For me, this transition was driven by an energy I've always carried—the need to move forward, resolve what was in front of me, and keep life organized and moving. I didn't spend much time questioning the contrast. My background in mathematics had trained me to think in systems, and systems can be applied anywhere. Whether in science, banking, or hospitality, the principles are similar: understand the structure, identify the variables, and bring order to the environment. I simply focused on what needed to be managed and returned to New Jersey. At the same time, there were practical matters to address. We had rented our home to an Italian family while we were away, and there was damage that needed to be repaired. I took care of that.

Professionally, the restaurant I stepped into was a very high-end establishment. It had a staff of more than twenty-five people, and I felt immediately comfortable. I had grown up in the restaurant business, and I had already managed restaurants part-time while working at the bank. In that sense, it was a natural fit. The work was demanding—long hours, physically taxing, and very hands-on. I was on my feet constantly. But I performed well, and the owner was extremely pleased. In fact, after a few months, the restaurant was forced to shut down due to misalignment with federal and state tax obligations. The owner later said publicly, in a newspaper interview, that he wished he had hired me from the beginning. That acknowledgment meant something to me.

Once again, I found myself looking for the next opportunity. The next weekend, while reading the New York Times, I came across an advertisement from Bloomberg Financial Markets. They were looking for mathematicians and scientists. I faxed my résumé to the headhunter listed in the ad. The next day, they called me. I interviewed on a Friday and was hired on the spot. I joined Bloomberg as a program manager, responsible for developing systems that captured trades entered on the Bloomberg Terminal and interfaced with banks' back-office systems. The role immediately reconnected me to my technical roots. Financially, the move also reflected progress with a starting salary of forty-one thousand dollars a year.

And, I would be working at Park Avenue and 59th Street, right in the heart of New York City.

I felt excited. Energized. Exhilarated.

This scene reinforces a recurring pattern: movement without fragmentation.

The external shifts—science to hospitality to finance—appear varied, yet the internal posture remains steady.

Structure, accountability, and composure remain consistent across environments.

The restaurant role becomes another system to stabilize—people, operations, pressure, cash flow, regulation.

The tools remain the same; the environment changes. Recognition from the owner, despite institutional failure, reinforces an emerging theme: performance is visible even when circumstances collapse.

The transition to Bloomberg illustrates preparedness meeting opportunity. Skills remain active during detours and continue compounding.

Capability continues unfolding across environments.

Key Takeaways

1. True leadership is transferable—when grounded in structure, responsibility, and respect for people, it adapts across industries.

2. Service excellence is not a role or sector; it is a discipline that builds trust wherever systems and humans intersect.

3. Career momentum grows from remaining staying prepared and visible, even during periods that appear to be detours.

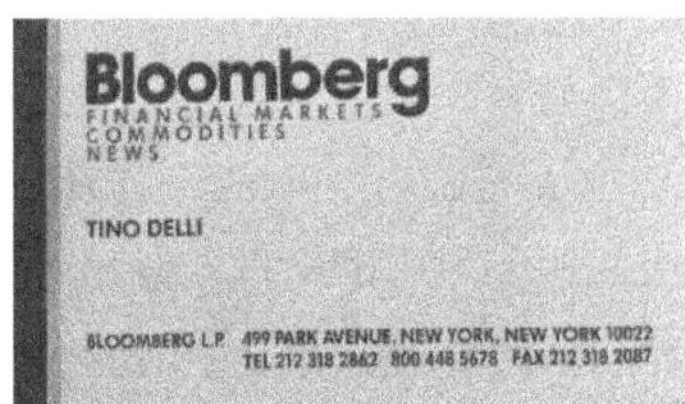

Q24

Joining Bloomberg placed you in the heart of Manhattan.

What was that experience like for you—both stepping into New York at that level and entering a company led by Michael Bloomberg?

Working in New York City, right in the middle of Manhattan, was exhilarating. Just before I started at Bloomberg, I had read a book about Michael Bloomberg and I knew his story—how he had left Salomon Brothers, founded his own company, and was building something entirely new. When I joined, the company was growing rapidly. At the time, Bloomberg occupied a single floor and was expanding to three floors. I arrived right at that inflection point. It felt like perfect timing. The energy was palpable—fast-moving, ambitious, and purpose-driven.

I stayed at Bloomberg for almost three years, and the experience was exceptional. I got to know Mike personally, along with the broader team. He became a mentor to me. From him, I learned the importance of building accurate, reliable, and fast systems; of putting clients first; and of delivering uncompromising service excellence. He surrounded himself with brilliant engineers and strong sales teams, and the culture emphasized intelligence, accountability, and trust.

Although I was hired for my technical skills and spent significant time coding and developing systems, the leadership team quickly recognized my ability to bridge people and technology. Because of my soft skills, I was often asked to accompany salespeople and analysts to meet with clients and gather data requirements. The systems I helped design eventually integrated trade capture for more than fifty banks globally, with institutions using the Bloomberg Terminal to route trades directly into their back-office systems. It was meaningful, high-impact work.

Bloomberg's culture extended beyond the office. Mike was remarkably generous and gracious with his team. He hosted company events—including private gatherings at his home upstate—complete with food, entertainment, and even a circus atmosphere. In the office, there was always food available: fruit, vegetables, and meals that reinforced a sense of care and community. He was, at his core, a humanitarian, and I connected deeply with that. We also shared a personal connection—our birthdays were just two days apart in February. I saw him regularly at events like the Corporate Challenge runs in Central Park, and those moments humanized leadership for me in a profound way.

During this time, people began sharing with me that I had the presence and temperament to work directly on a trading floor. I kept hearing it—and my curiosity grew. I enjoyed working behind the scenes, but I felt drawn to being closer to the action. At the same time, my relationship with my immediate manager became strained. She was not particularly supportive of the group dynamics, and I began to feel neglected. Looking back, I can see that I was also immature in how I handled the situation. Eventually, a headhunter contacted me. Bankers Trust—known today as Deutsche Bank—was looking for an Assistant Vice President with my background. Coming from Bloomberg carried significant weight. At the time, I was earning fifty-one thousand dollars and I had accumulated about the same amount in deferred bonus certificates that would vest if I stayed another year. Bankers Trust offered me, with a sign on bonus, one-hundred thousand dollars to start.

I accepted immediately. I didn't give Bloomberg a full two weeks' notice, and that is something I regret. Mike was upset and asked to meet with me. He wanted to understand why I was leaving. I told him simply that I wanted to work on Wall Street. In hindsight, I wish I had handled that transition with more maturity. I should have been more transparent about the internal challenges I was facing and more respectful of the relationship we had built. Looking back now, I might have stayed longer at Bloomberg if I had approached things differently. I truly enjoyed working with Mike and his team. Years later, when I authored my book, I sent Mike a copy while he was serving as mayor. He wrote back to me. That acknowledgment stayed with me.

Still, I was excited. Bankers Trust was located directly across from the World Trade Center, and the opportunity to work on a live trading floor felt like stepping into the center of global finance—another powerful chapter waiting to unfold.

Reflections

This scene marks acceleration with integration.

Prior experiences—mathematics, banking discipline, hospitality, scientific precision—converge a scale.

Bloomberg becomes the environment where structure, service, and technology operate simultaneously and visibly. The proximity to Michael Bloomberg adds another layer: leadership modeled through clarity, standards, and expectation. Excellence becomes operational—clear, measurable, and practiced daily.

Recognition of the author's ability to bridge systems and people signals a recurring strength—translation. Not just coding systems, but aligning technical architecture with human need.

The decision to leave introduces an important tension: ambition was accelerating ahead of full relational awareness. Capability was expanding, and experience was still maturing.

This moment honors what was built and reveals an important lesson—acceleration without full alignment carries consequence, even in success.

Key Takeaways

1. Technical excellence becomes transformational when paired with service and humanity.

2. The ability to translate between people and systems is a rare and durable leadership advantage.

3. The manner in which a chapter closes shapes the integrity of what follows.

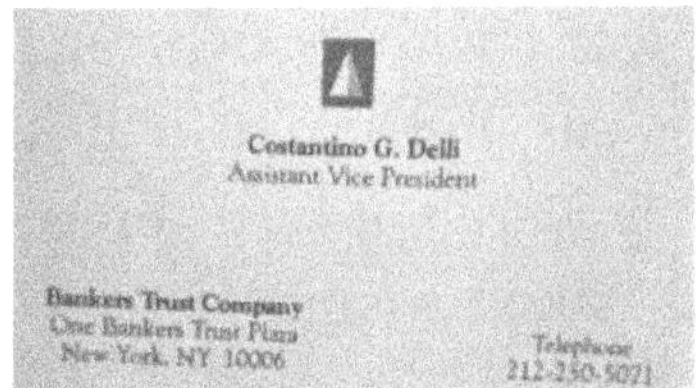

Q25

Joining a major Wall Street bank placed you inside one of the most demanding environments imaginable. At the same time, your mother was still living with you.

How did you balance those two worlds?

By the time I began working on Wall Street, my mother was doing much better. She had found a part-time job caring for twin boys at a pastry shop in our Trenton neighborhood, which gave her structure, purpose, and connection. Knowing she was more stable made it possible for me to fully commit to the intensity of my work.

Prior to joining the bank, I was still commuting daily. My days began before sunrise and often didn't end until after eight at night. With this new role, I was able to afford and rent an apartment in Battery Park City. The area had several beautiful new high-rise buildings, and I could walk directly to work on Wall Street. That change alone altered my quality of life significantly.

The work itself was exhilarating and demanding. I was managing and supporting a trading and sales desk in the bond market. Our team was small—just three of us—and everyone was highly technical. What distinguished me was not just technical competence, but polish, presence, and service orientation. I understood how to work with traders and salespeople, how to anticipate their needs, and how to deliver solutions efficiently and reliably. They were not accustomed to that level of proactive service, and I stood out quickly.

I developed several systems programmatically and loved the pace and intensity of working directly with traders. We were also involved in projects with the federal government, including the implementation of a new bond auction system. When issues arose on the government's side, there was pressure from leadership to explain why the system hadn't worked on day one—despite the fact that our team had tested everything thoroughly and was fully prepared. In one instance, I called a federal official and asked if he could at least put in writing that the issue originated on their side and my team wouldn't be unfairly blamed. He admitted the problem but said he couldn't put it in writing for political reasons.

Even so, I documented the interaction carefully—noting that the conversation had taken place on a recorded trading desk line. That was how I protected the team. I learned to anticipate risk before it surfaced. The pressure was relentless. My blood pressure rose to dangerous levels—a clear physiological signal that the pace carried cost. At the same time, something else was becoming clear: I was exceptional at service excellence. It became increasingly clear that I carried a rare combination of technical depth and human understanding— the kind that naturally lends itself to independent advisory work.

During my twelve-month review, my managing director said something I've never forgotten: "If there were ever a fire, I would want you in it with me, because I know you'd get me out safely." Yet she didn't want to give me a raise. Her concern was that I wasn't the "perfect technical fit." In hindsight, the real issue was that the trading group gravitated toward me. They came to me for solutions, and the rest of the team felt overshadowed. Eventually, we parted ways. I received a three-month severance.

Looking back now, my mind often returns to my first week there. I had just moved into my apartment in Battery Park City—right around my birthday in February. Within days, the World Trade Center bombing took place in the underground garage beneath the towers, directly across from our building. That day the office was tense and confusing. We were told to remain inside, and information was limited. I was so immersed in the work that I didn't fully grasp what had happened until later that evening when I left the building and saw the chaos outside. Looking back, that moment almost felt like an early signal—an uneasy beginning to a chapter that would ultimately prove shorter than expected.

Less than a month later, a new opportunity appeared. Valinor Inc., founded by two brothers, were looking to open a New York City office and build out a consulting practice. They were a Microsoft-certified provider and wanted me to lead the expansion. I negotiated a starting compensation of one-hundred and fifty-thousand dollars a year—a fifty-percent increase I had secured two years earlier.

The work began taking me internationally—first to London, and then to other parts of Europe. It was my first exposure to operating across borders, cultures, and financial centers. That experience expanded my perspective and quietly marked the beginning of a more global way of thinking about work, systems, and leadership.

Reflections

This scene represents acceleration at scale.

Inside the trading floor environment, leadership expresses itself functionally rather than formally.

Influence is earned through composure under pressure, anticipatory thinking, and disciplined protection of others.

What distinguishes this period is protective intelligence.

Technical capability is present, but it is the ability to translate risk, document exposure, and shield teams from political fallout that builds trust.

Service becomes structural. At the same time, misalignment begins to surface. Recognition increases. Influence expands.

Formal authority lags behind contribution. That tension reveals an important truth: systems sometimes struggle to recognize the behaviors that stabilize them.

The body registers what ambition overlooks. Rising blood pressure becomes a signal—an early warning from the body. Performance continues, even as internal equilibrium narrows.

The seeds of autonomy are planted here through expanding structural awareness.

Independence begins emerging as a natural expression of alignment.

Key Takeaways

1. Service excellence becomes leadership when it protects others under pressure.

2. Being highly capable in misaligned systems often signals readiness for independence.

3. Physical stress is frequently the earliest indicator that evolution is required.

Q26

The pace, responsibility, and opportunity were all converging. Was this your true entry into consulting?

That's exactly right—this was my true entry into consulting. It felt like a powerful opportunity, not only for me, but for the firm. They were missing a level of service excellence that their clients were actively complaining about. Projects were failing not because of lack of intelligence, but because delivery, communication, and alignment were breaking down. I stepped in and did what I instinctively do: I put out fires. I stabilized relationships. I rebuilt trust.

We were working with several banks, and I became the connective tissue between clients and delivery teams. The work expanded quickly. I was flying to Frankfurt, traveling to London, and at the same time managing a team of more than ten consultants—system developers, infrastructure specialists, and system-integration professionals. The work was excellent. I had strong relationships with the two brothers who owned the firm, and I felt respected. Professionally, I was fully utilizing my technical background while operating at a leadership level. This was consulting— real consulting—and I was thriving in it.

At the same time, my personal life was accelerating just as quickly. I had moved uptown and living on Park Avenue, in a triplex apartment at 54th and Park. Everything felt dynamic, expansive, and alive. I had also begun dating a beautiful Black woman—an actress and model. Our relationship intensified quickly. During that time, I also brought her home to meet my mother. I was still checking in regularly, making sure my mother was doing well and that life at home remained steady. Even as my work and personal life accelerated, that sense of responsibility toward her never left me.

Around that same period, the brothers introduced a new bonus structure for the following year and asked me to commit to generating a specific revenue target—without any historical baseline to support it. As I reviewed the terms, the structure felt incoherent and unrealistic. When I raised my concerns, the conversation became tense. That following weekend, everything seemed to collide. I took my girlfriend to a diner where she surprised me by proposing and offering me a ring. I was touched and overwhelmed—I shared that I needed time to reflect. Later that evening, I was rushed to the hospital for severe food poisoning from contaminated eggs in the meal we had eaten at the diner earlier. The incident was later reported in the newspaper after several people became ill. I was hospitalized and unable to work for several days.

My employer interpreted the absence differently. Coming so soon after the confrontation about the revenue targets, they assumed I was using the illness as an excuse. When I returned, they told me not to come back. Suddenly, I had lost the job I loved. The relationship felt misaligned. I was emotionally overloaded, physically depleted, disoriented. I sat on my apartment floor at two in the morning, crying uncontrollably—a breaking point. In that stillness, a quiet voice emerged: "Find me."

Reflections

This scene marks a structural rupture.

Until now, competence, discipline, and adaptability had carried every transition. Here, external acceleration outpaces internal coherence. Professional authority expands. Personal pressure intensifies. Physical limits surface.

The collapse is multidimensional—career disruption, relational misalignment, bodily depletion. What had previously been managed through effort now calls for deeper integration. The quiet instruction to "Find me" signals a fundamental shift.

The center of gravity begins to move inward. Integration becomes necessary. From this point forward, success will require alignment between capability, values, and identity.

The architecture of a philosophy begins as a response to imbalance.

Key Takeaways

1. Acceleration without coherence eventually exposes structural misalignment.

2. Capability can build momentum; alignment sustains it.

3. Rupture often marks the beginning of integration rather than the end of success.

CHAPTER FIVE

Integration in Motion

Creativity, Enterprise, Love—and Authorship

Q27

*After the breakdown and the moment you heard "Find me"—
what unfolded?*

What followed the breakdown was a reconnection to a part of
me that had always existed—silence.

My days slowed. The urgency fell away. Mornings became
deliberate. And in that stillness, I was no longer reacting—I
was observing. One of my greatest teachers during that period
was my small white Pekingese, Bianco. Every morning around
six, he would wake up with unmistakable joy. He'd run outside
into the backyard, stop at every flower, every corner, every
scent—fully present, completely absorbed in the moment.
Watching him reminded me of something I had forgotten: life
is not lived ahead of us or behind us, but exactly where we are.
That presence mattered.

I began to write and to empty my mind. Journaling became a
daily ritual. And silence emerged gradually. I started reading
poetry, sitting with language rather than analyzing it. I spent
more time in nature, paid attention to what I ate, moved, and
slept. I learned about meditation and committed to it as a daily

practice. As layers peeled away, I started to see the pattern of my life with clarity. I had always delivered value and been effective. But my success had been inconsistent in one critical way: it was not anchored. I was excelling outwardly while neglecting a sustained connection inwardly. When pressure mounted, I disconnected from myself—and when that happened, imbalance followed. That was the missing piece.

During that period, something familiar began to surface. It was a reconnection and returning to "home"—a part of myself that had always been present but not fully embodied. In the stillness, I recognized that sustainable excellence required a living connection to what I named the *Creative Optimum Self*— the dimension of being that operates with clarity, presence, intuition, and integrity.

Through reflection, I identified five inner practices that kept me connected to that state: journaling, meditation, inspirational reading, time in nature and solitude, intentional nutrition, and caring for the body. These were grounding practices that kept me aligned and centered. From there, I recognized that inner alignment alone was not enough. The world still required action. As a result, I identified five outer practices, drawn from everything I had learned in business and leadership: executing with clarity, nurturing relationships, tying up loose ends, operating with warmth and grace, and applying creativity to problem-solving.

Music also played an important role in that reconstruction. From the time I arrived in the United States as a boy, music had always been a constant presence in my life. Early on I listened to the classic rock my brother loved—bands like Boston and Led Zeppelin—then over the years I found myself deeply drawn to the soulful power of disco, R&B and rhythm-driven music. Artists like Lionel Richie, the Commodores, Earth, Wind & Fire, Michael Jackson, Luther Vandross, and Neil Diamond became part of the soundtrack of my life. Alongside this, Italian music remained a quiet influence—artists like Andrea Bocelli and Eros Ramazzotti, and more recently Malika Ayane, whose blend of soul, R&B, and pop brings that connection into the present.

During difficult periods especially, music had a way of steadying me, lifting my energy, and reconnecting me with something deeper. As I rebuilt myself, I began using music more consciously—sometimes meditation music to support stillness, other times soulful music that carried emotion and vitality. I also noticed something else: the deep connection between music and mathematics. Rhythm, timing, and harmony follow patterns that mirror the structure of the universe itself. Listening while I worked or reflected helped me enter a state of flow where thought, intuition, and creativity aligned. In its own way, music became another pathway back to my Creative Optimum Self.

When practiced together, the Inner and Outer Steps formed a complete system—a way of living that kept action rooted in awareness, and ambition guided by presence. For the first time, my life made sense as a whole. What had felt like collapse revealed itself as a correction. I hadn't failed—I had drifted away from myself. And now, I was returning. That realization would later become the foundation of my work, my writing, and eventually my philosophy. But at the time, it was simpler than that. I had found my way back to center.

At the same time, something unexpected happened. My ex-girlfriend had sent my headshot to agents, just to see if anything might come of it. A few days later, I was contacted by

J. Michael Bloom Associates—one of the top agencies in New York City. Suddenly, I was being sent out on commercial auditions, including for Olive Garden and other national brands. For about six months, that became my rhythm. I auditioned. I wrote, reflected and listened. I did background work on television shows, landed a recurring background role on a soap opera, and appeared in other series. One of the Olive Garden commercials ran extensively, with multiple versions produced over time. As a principal performer, I qualified for and joined the Screen Actors Guild. It was a deeply creative period—expressive, exploratory, and healing.

One small moment from that period stayed with me in a way I never fully understood. One afternoon after filming a recurring background role on the ABC soap opera *The City*, I was leaving the studio on Manhattan's Upper West Side. As I stepped outside, two older gentlemen—both probably in their sixties—approached me with big smiles and asked for my autograph. I was surprised. I wasn't famous, just a background actor beginning to explore something new. Still, I gladly signed my name—my stage name Cos Dellin—and asked who I should make it out to.

"Angelo," one said.

"Santo," said the other.

Angel and Saint. I smiled at the coincidence, handed the paper back, and began walking toward the river. The studio entrance was secure behind me, and the only way out was the path I had taken. After about thirty seconds, still amused by their names, I turned around to look back. They were gone. Completely gone.

I never saw them again.

Even now, that moment stays with me. At a time when my life had slowed and my attention had deepened, it felt almost like a quiet affirmation—one of those small mysteries life sometimes offers when we begin listening more closely.

Reflections

This scene marks the first conscious integration point in the narrative.

For the first time, movement turns inward before it moves outward.

The collapse produces stillness.

Stillness produces awareness.

Awareness produces structure.

Presence re-enters through ordinary rituals—morning light, a dog moving through the garden, breath without urgency. Nothing dramatic is required. Coherence returns through attention.

Music also revealed something deeper. Rhythm, harmony, and mathematical structure mirror the underlying order of the universe itself. Listening became another form of alignment— where intuition, creativity, and logic moved together in quiet coherence.

The articulation of inner and outer practices signals maturation. Performance is no longer separated from awareness. Action begins to arise from alignment rather than compensation.

The creative reawakening through acting becomes a form of expansion and expression. It restores dimensions of identity that achievement alone had quieted.

The architecture becomes intentional here.

my movie

Key Takeaways

1. Sustainable leadership requires internal coherence; without it, achievement becomes unstable under pressure.

2. Outer excellence compounds when it is rooted in disciplined inner recalibration.

3. Creative expression restores wholeness and often reveals identity beyond professional achievement.

Q28

After reconnecting with yourself in that period of silence and creative exploration, how did you begin expanding your life and work again?

While I was writing, acting, reflecting, and rebuilding from the inside out, I still needed to support myself. I accepted a role with Wilco Systems as a senior consultant and project manager, even at a lower salary. The work took me internationally—to London and Greece—and once again, I delivered results, built trust, and operated at a high level. But this time, something was different. I wasn't overextending. Or abandoning myself. I was applying the same inner principles I had been cultivating—presence, clarity, alignment—directly into my professional work.

After a few months, the company's president, Roy Staines, sat down with me and said words I had heard before, but now heard differently: "You're very talented. The way you operate—you should have your own consulting practice." This time, it didn't feel like advice. It felt like confirmation. I opened COS Enterprises Inc. and the name COS had emerged during my creative period. It reflected a deeper clarity I had reconnected with—the Creative Optimum Self: the part of us that operates before fear, conditioning, and noise take over. For consulting, COS became Creative Optimum Solutions—the same inner Source, now applied outwardly to organizations, systems, and leadership challenges. I approached the launch methodically: incorporation, structure, business cards, networking.

At the same time, I was equally committed to staying creatively alive. I continued studying acting in New York—at HB Studio and auditioning for The Actor's Studio. For the audition, I selected a scene from *Barefoot in the Park*. I played Robert Redford's role opposite a scene partner, performing a romantic comedic exchange originally portrayed by Redford and Jane Fonda. It was a late Saturday evening. Three senior judges sat before us—quiet, reserved, visibly fatigued from a long day of auditions. We performed our ten-minute scene fully committed. When it ended, the room was silent. No applause or commentary as it was customary. Yet as we exited, I noticed something unmistakable—the three men were smiling, almost glowing. I felt exhilarated. I had entertained them and moved "something" in the room.

Later, a teacher remarked that I had a natural ability to embody Redford's spirit—calm strength, restraint, intelligence beneath simplicity. That observation stayed with me. The following year, I wrote Bob a twelve-page letter— part memoir, part reflection—sharing my life from Italy to that present moment. I described how my journey seemed to mirror the emotional architecture of many of the characters he had portrayed: men navigating courage, solitude, moral tension, and quiet resilience. It felt like a kindred recognition across distance. He responded—through correspondence sent on his behalf—acknowledging my writing and my interest in working with him. There was gracious exchange back and forth over time. My headshots were requested and dialogue remained open. The connection brought me back to our journey to America years earlier, when I watched *The Way We Were* on the plane. I felt and still feel today that he was a kindred spirit.

Over time, the creative work supported my consulting—it sharpened my presence, emotional intelligence, intuition, and ability to read people and systems. My first consulting engagement came with Guardian Insurance in New York City. I supported their Project Management Office, bringing structure, governance, and clarity to a fragmented environment. It was the ideal first client—disciplined execution anchored in purpose.

From the beginning, COS was a consulting practice based on the outward expression of an inner alignment—creativity and consulting evolving together.

Reflections

This scene marks the first external proof that inner alignment can operate within real-world pressure.

Practical work returns—travel, delivery, clients, accountability—but the posture has evolved. Execution now moves together with self-connection. The same technical rigor remains present, grounded in awareness and balance.

The comment from the company president lands differently because the foundation has matured. Earlier in life, similar words might have sparked acceleration. Now they affirm readiness. Entrepreneurship begins to take shape as a natural extension of coherence.

The naming of COS reflects this shift. It is articulation catching up to embodiment. The creative and the operational move together as integrated competencies.

The Redford audition becomes symbolic. Presence, restraint, and quiet authority are explored artistically before they appear professionally. Performance becomes preparation for leadership.

The Redford correspondence becomes a quiet affirmation. Recognition from a figure who embodied courage, moral tension, and restrained strength reflects the same architecture forming within the author.

The first client becomes a demonstration of integration. Governance, structure, and disciplined execution operate together with presence. What begins to take shape is a consulting practice guided by a simple architecture: clarity inward, precision outward.

Key Takeaways

1. Alignment proves itself when applied under real-world pressure.

2. Entrepreneurship rooted in coherence sustains momentum without self-abandonment.

3. Integration of creativity and structure produces durable leadership.

Q29

What did those early years of consulting reveal to you about leadership, systems, and yourself?

What I began to recognize during those early consulting years was that everything in my life had been quietly building toward a coherent philosophy—something revealing itself through lived experience. At the center of it all was the Creative Optimum Self—a deeper Source of clarity and intelligence that remains available beneath conditioning and distraction. As I reflected more deeply, I realized that this Source expresses itself through distinct, interdependent components.

First, there is the inner world—our emotional landscape, intuition, values, and sense of meaning. Then there is the body—the physical vessel that must be cared for, respected, and aligned, because without health and vitality, nothing else sustains itself. Then comes the mind—the cognitive and creative intelligence that allows us to think clearly, architect frameworks, solve problems, and bring order to complexity. Those three dimensions—inner world, body, and mind— must be aligned first. Only then can the fourth dimension fully emerge: how we apply ourselves outwardly through our work—how we lead, consult, design systems, and serve organizations and people. And finally, the fifth dimension extends beyond the immediate workplace—our impact on the broader world, on culture, on legacy, and on others we may never meet.

Over time, I came to understand that when those five dimensions operate in coherence, leadership becomes intelligent in a deeper way. I name this Integrated Leadership Intelligence—the disciplined capacity to align inner clarity, physical vitality, cognitive precision, professional execution, and broader impact into a single operating system. It was the Creative Optimum Self expressing itself outwardly in structured environments.

This is how the COS philosophy truly took shape—an integrated way of living and working. My creative process— acting studies, journaling, meditation—was deeply connected to my leadership and consulting work. It was *supporting it*. At the same time, my consulting work gave real-world structure and validation to what I was discovering internally. Everything began aligning naturally.

During this period, something else meaningful happened. In New York City, I unexpectedly reconnected someone I had known when I was seventeen and hadn't seen in many years. It was the "young princess" who had once gotten away. The reconnection felt deeply serendipitous—occurring right in the midst of my professional momentum, at one of my client sites. It felt as though life was reflecting back what was happening internally: my inner world becoming more balanced and coherent, my outer world responding through meaningful work, my creative life supporting my presence and leadership, and my personal relationships aligning with greater authenticity. For the first time, nothing felt fragmented. Everything belonged.

Reflections

This moment marks the articulation of what had long been lived.

What began as intuitive integration across body, mind, inner life, work, and impact is now expressed clearly in language.

The model emerges as a way to describe something already demonstrated through experience and pressure.

The significance lies in its timing.

This recognition arrives after decades of movement across industries, roles, responsibility, collapse, and renewal.

The articulation reflects maturity and lived understanding.

Integrated Leadership Intelligence becomes a way to describe how coherence across dimensions produces durability in action.

It captures the conditions that sustain clarity, resilience, and performance over time.

Experience evolves into framework.

Framework becomes transferable.

Here, lived pattern becomes articulated philosophy.

Key Takeaways

1. Sustainable leadership emerges when inner coherence guides external influence.

2. Systems perform best when body, mind, and values operate as interconnected dimensions.

3. Enduring philosophy grows from lived integration expressed through experience.

Q30

It sounds like many parts of your life were finally coming into alignment—your work, your inner world, your sense of purpose, and even a meaningful reconnection from your past.

Did it feel like life was finally moving forward in a more natural way?

Yes—for the first time, life felt aligned rather than forced.

Professionally, my consulting work had entered a more mature phase. I began taking on senior-level engagements, including work with Citibank, where I was exposed to complex enterprise environments and higher-stakes decision-making. That progression continued into a long-term engagement with Ziff Davis Media, where my role expanded significantly.

At Ziff Davis, I worked closely with C-suite executives during a critical period leading up to Y2K. My focus was business continuity planning—preparing leadership teams and boards for systemic risk, operational resilience, and crisis response. That work brought me into executive and board-level meetings, where clarity, trust, and composure mattered as much as technical expertise. It was no longer just about delivering projects; it was about stewarding confidence at the highest levels of an organization. I was entrusted with managing multiple external consulting resources—including senior professionals from major global advisory firms—aligning their efforts within the broader enterprise program. My client relied on me for strategy, execution, alignment and coordination of high-level consulting talent across the initiative. That trust signaled a new level of credibility in my leadership.

At the same time, my personal life felt equally grounded. My relationship with my girlfriend deepened with a sense of ease and shared history. My mother was finally settled—we sold our family home and moved her into a senior apartment home by the Jersey Shore—by the ocean as she had always dreamed. Knowing she was safe, independent, and at peace closed a long emotional loop for me.

With that foundation in place, my curiosity expanded again—this time toward film, not just as an actor, but as a producer. The shift felt natural. Producing drew on the same strengths I had developed in consulting: structuring complex initiatives, aligning creative and operational stakeholders, managing risk, and guiding projects from vision to execution. I began studying producing with intention, recognizing it as a convergence point between creativity and business.

Around that time, I began learning more about Sherry Lansing's journey—her early acting career, her analytical background, and her rise into studio leadership at Paramount Pictures. Her path resonated deeply with me. I reached out and shared pieces of my writing—reflections that blended creativity, leadership, and lived experience.

She responded personally, expressing appreciation for the cinematic quality of the writing and noting the balance between creative instinct and business discipline. She recognized in me a rare combination that translated naturally into producing. Through that correspondence, she connected me with her right-hand person, Brad Kessell, Vice President of Creative Services at Paramount Pictures. Brad invited me to meet with him when I was in Hollywood to explore potential opportunities with the studio.

My girlfriend and I decided to travel to L.A. together as an exploration. We wanted to expand possibilities: consulting, creative work, and continued acting and producing studies. I felt ready to leave my New Jersey "nest." My mother was settled. Momentum was guided by alignment, curiosity, and confidence.

Reflections

This scene marks the transition from performance to stewardship.

Consulting evolves from delivery to executive counsel. The work shifts upward in altitude—into rooms where uncertainty, risk, and perception must be managed alongside systems and execution.

Leadership here is measured through composure, discernment, and the ability to steady others amid uncertainty.

Simultaneously, creativity ceases to be parallel and becomes integrated. Producing reflects the same underlying architecture as consulting: aligning stakeholders, managing complexity, translating vision into structured execution.

Personal responsibility resolves. Professional credibility stabilizes. Curiosity expands without fragmentation.

Key Takeaways

1. Leadership matures when responsibility shifts from execution to stewardship, where clarity must be held amid uncertainty.

2. Creative and analytical intelligence operate powerfully together. When integrated, they allow leaders to navigate complexity and ambiguity with confidence.

3. True alignment creates momentum without urgency. Sustainable growth emerges when inner stability supports outer expansion.

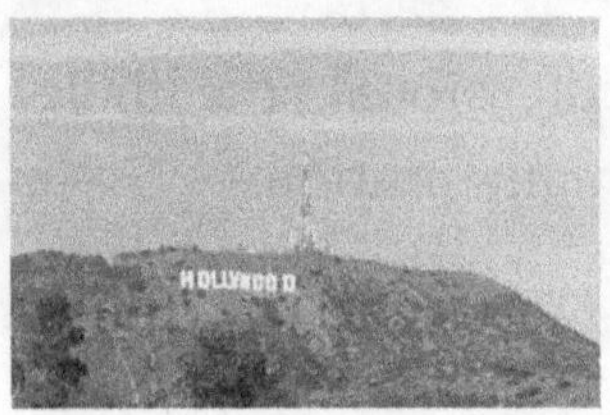

Q31

You traveled to Los Angeles with a thoughtful sense of direction and openness to possibility.

How did that chapter of your journey unfold?

It turned out to be deeply meaningful—even more than I could have imagined, unfolding in ways that surprised me. I loved Los Angeles from the very beginning. The climate reminded me of Taranto, Italy. The ocean, the light, the openness—it felt like I had come home to a place I didn't know I had been missing. The creative energy was immediate. I began journaling daily, intensely. In fact, I went back and started documenting my entire life from the beginning. That practice never stopped. To this day, those journals span over two thousand pages.

Creatively, things were flowing. We found a remarkable acting teacher, Lilyan Chauvin, whose career included numerous film and television roles, including alongside Leonardo DiCaprio in *Catch Me If You Can*. The work with Lilyan helped me stay grounded, open, and expressive. At the same time, I began to understand that the entertainment industry is highly insulated. Entering it requires deep relationships, patience, and persistence.

True to her word, Sherry arranged for me to meet with Brad Kessell at Paramount Pictures. When I first walked onto the Paramount lot to meet him, something unexpected happened inside me. The moment I stepped through the gates, I felt an immediate sense of familiarity—as if I had entered a place I had known for a long time. The sound stages, the energy, the quiet movement of people creating stories—it felt alive. I had spent my whole life watching films that came out of places like this, and standing there I felt something very simple and very clear: I belonged in that environment.

Brad appreciated my business background, the creativity reflected in my letters to Sherry, and my desire to contribute to the industry. Although I had no producer credits yet, we discussed possible ways I could begin positioning myself. It was clear the path would require time, patience, and the right opportunities.

Then September 11th happened.

That moment changed everything—for all of us. Perspective shifted overnight. What mattered, what felt urgent, what felt permanent—all of it was suddenly seen through a different lens. We were in New Jersey visiting when it happened, and we remained there for some time. When the towers fell, the event was deeply personal for me. I had spent countless nights at the Marriott inside the World Trade Center—working late, staying overnight, sharing meals, building relationships with people who knew me by name. Bankers Trust, where I had worked earlier in my career, stood directly across the street. These were not distant landmarks. They were part of my life. Friends were lost that day. People I knew. Places I had walked through many times disappeared in hours. Watching the events unfold from New Jersey was devastating. It felt as if a piece of the world I knew had vanished. In that moment, ambition lost its urgency. Presence, safety, family, and meaning came sharply into focus. The experience did not derail my path. It clarified it.

When we eventually returned to Los Angeles, the momentum had slowed significantly. Projects paused. Energy shifted. The industry felt different. After nearly a year, my girlfriend had an opportunity back in New Jersey—a potential role in public television, in broadcasting. At the same time, I realized that my path with Paramount would require more time than we could realistically give it right then. And another force was present: my mother. She was alone, and that protective instinct—the one I've carried my whole life—resurfaced. It was the longest I had ever been away from her, and something in me knew it was time to return.

Just before we left Los Angeles, something unexpected happened—almost like a parting gift. I was called in to audition for a feature role in the HBO film *Live from Baghdad*, starring Michael Keaton and Helena Bonham Carter. The role was originally written without lines—an Italian cashier. The symmetry wasn't lost on me; it echoed being five years old in my parents' café. During the audition, I improvised—speaking Italian in a scene with Michael and Helena. The moment came alive. Director Mick Jackson responded immediately, adding dialogue to the role. I was given dialogue, received screen credit, and stepped onto a professional set in a fully realized way.

It felt like Hollywood saying goodbye, temporarily at least, but I knew I would return.

Reflections

This scene unfolds as discernment under historical rupture.

Los Angeles initially represents expansion—creative exploration aligned with professional maturity.

The environment feels intuitive, almost ancestral in climate and rhythm.

Creative discipline deepens through journaling and study, signaling integration and maturity.

September 11th alters the emotional architecture of the moment.

The shift is existential.

Landmarks become personal. Memory becomes immediate.

Velocity loses priority. Presence gains weight.

This period reflects calibration rather than retreat. Creative identity remains alive.

Professional opportunity remains present. Responsibility and meaning reorder the hierarchy of choice.

The return east reflects continuity of character—the same protective instinct, values hierarchy, and integrated decision-making.

This moment reinforces a pattern: ambition advances when coherence remains intact.

Key Takeaways

1. Alignment is tested during disruption, when values take priority over ambition.

2. Creative practice strengthens leadership by preserving clarity under uncertainty.

3. Discernment—the ability to recalibrate direction without losing identity—is a defining leadership trait.

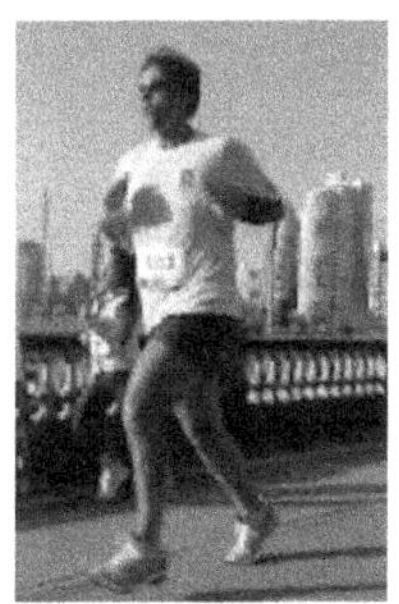

Q32

After that experience in Los Angeles, when you returned home, did it change the trajectory of your life? Did you come back with new clarity or discoveries about yourself?

Returning from Los Angeles marked a quiet but decisive turning point. One of the clearest realizations that emerged during that period was how deeply the role of caretaker had shaped my life. I had been supporting my mother since childhood—emotionally, practically, and instinctively—and over time, that same dynamic had extended into my adult relationships. I began to see a recurring pattern: a natural tendency to protect, stabilize, and provide—often without fully recognizing the cost to my own emotional equilibrium. That awareness brought new clarity to my relationship with my girlfriend.

When we reconnected after many years, I realized that we were arriving with different expectations. I had romanticized the connection—seeing her as "the one who got away"—a symbol from an earlier chapter of my life. In truth, what she may have been seeking was something gentler and more grounded: a deep friendship, a reconnection rooted in familiarity rather than projection. Recognizing that difference was not easy. But parting ways felt necessary—and ultimately respectful—for both of us. It was an important lesson in discernment: learning to release relationships with honesty rather than force.

At the same time, my responsibility toward my mother remained present, but it began to take a new form. She was living independently, yet required closer supervision. Coincidentally, an assisted living community was being built next door to her residence—an option I quietly noted as part of a longer-term plan. I knew I needed to return to work and allow creative opportunities—including those connected to Paramount Pictures—the time they required to unfold. With that clarity, I made the decision to return to New York City— a place that had always felt like home.

Soon after, I secured a senior consulting engagement with JPMorgan Chase. The work was substantial and highly visible: I was involved in a large-scale transformation initiative tied to a multi-billion-dollar outsourcing program with IBM, during a pivotal period when JPMorgan and Bank One were merging and Jamie Dimon had just stepped into the CEO role. As part of that initiative, I was entrusted with overseeing and coordinating senior IBM consulting teams embedded in the program. At the request of executive leadership, including Jamie Dimon, our team was asked to assess whether the multi-billion-dollar outsourcing strategy should proceed as structured or be reconsidered.

After a comprehensive evaluation of operational, financial, and long-term strategic implications, I was among the senior consultants who recommended that key capabilities remain in-house. Jamie ultimately accepted that recommendation. That moment signaled a new level of trust and influence— advising at scale, with decisions that carried enterprise-wide consequence.

Personally, it allowed me to reestablish independence— including moving into my own apartment on the Upper West Side—while continuing to plan responsibly for my mother's future. The pieces felt aligned in a sustainable way: care without overextension, work without self-abandonment, and progress without urgency.

Reflections

This scene reveals maturation through pattern recognition.

The return from Los Angeles integrates the creative awakening within a broader life context. What becomes visible is a lifelong caretaker identity, formed early and carried forward into adult relationships and professional dynamics.

The recognition reflects growth in awareness. Patterns that once operated unconsciously now become visible. Responsibility becomes deliberate.

Responsibility evolves from instinctive overextension into conscious choice. Relationships begin to reflect alignment and sustainability. Protection remains present, expressed with discernment and balance.

Professionally, the move into a complex transformation initiative at JPMorgan Chase mirrors this evolution. The scale expands. The stakes rise. The posture becomes steadier.

Leadership expresses itself through composure and clarity, while care for others remains grounded in personal equilibrium.

Key Takeaways

1. Roles formed early in life often continue shaping leadership until they are brought into conscious awareness.

2. Responsibility matures when guided by healthy boundaries and thoughtful discernment.

3. Sustainable authority grows when care for others is supported by self-respect and inner stability.

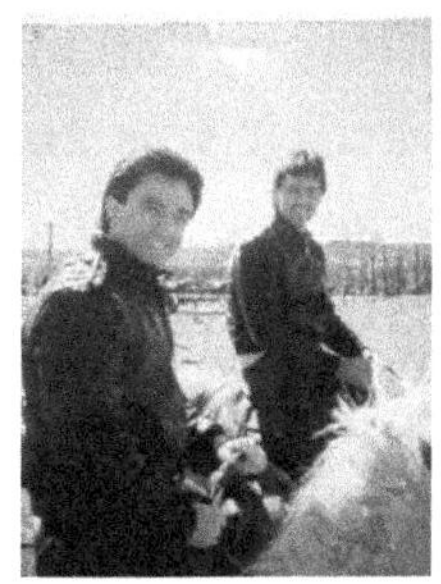

Q33

As your life settled into a new rhythm after returning to New York, how did that period begin to unfold— professionally and personally?

Returning to New York marked a period of quiet consolidation.

Professionally, my engagement with JPMorgan Chase continued to expand as a result of the trust established during the earlier transformation work. The assignment extended and evolved, leading to additional responsibilities, including supporting the Private Banking Group through major infrastructure upgrades and application modernization. The work was complex and highly visible, requiring coordination across senior stakeholders and multiple technical teams. It demanded composure, judgment, and sustained focus—and I was fully engaged in it.

Around that same period, something meaningful resurfaced from Los Angeles. Following my earlier meetings, I was invited back for a follow-up conversation with Brad Kessell at

Paramount Pictures. During that discussion, I was offered a path to step in as a producer—developing and pitching story ideas, with the possibility of being based on the lot and paired with a screenwriter if a concept moved forward. It was an opportunity I took seriously. I had always been a strong writer, and storytelling had become a natural extension of my creative and strategic thinking. But at that moment, my responsibilities were firmly rooted in New York—my work at JPMorgan, and my commitment to my mother. I said I would reflect and follow up when the timing was right. Ultimately, I didn't pursue it further. And when Sherry Lansing retired, I reached out to wish her well. Looking back, I recognize that timing—not talent—was the determining factor. I've learned that some doors do not close; they wait for alignment.

At the same time, my life had a different rhythm than before. On weekends, I returned home to New Jersey to spend time with my mother, making sure she was stable and supported. She was more independent now, but still needed presence and care. That balance—focused professional intensity during the week, grounded family responsibility on the weekends— became my steady pattern for over a year. There was also a reconnection unfolding quietly with my brother. We had always been close growing up, but after he married, he had distanced himself from the family. During this period, he was going through a divorce, and I was there for him—listening, supporting, and hoping that our bond could be rebuilt. That time together mattered.

Personally, I wasn't rushing anything. I dated casually, stayed social, but remained anchored in my work, my routines, and my inner practices. I felt centered, productive, and stable— not searching, not forcing, simply living. Then, shortly before my birthday, something subtle shifted. While journaling one evening, I found myself writing about the kind of woman I hoped to meet—guided by clarity and quiet confidence. I wrote about someone vibrant and alive, warm, present, and capable of sharing life as a true partner. I closed the journal without expectation. On Valentine's night, in the laundry room of my apartment building, I met the woman I had been writing about.

I didn't know it then—but that moment would open the next chapter of my life.

Reflections

This scene reflects consolidation and integration.

Professional influence deepens quietly—enterprise decisions shaped with composure and authority expressed without spectacle.

The Paramount invitation introduces creative possibility, while discernment and timing guide the response.

Opportunity is considered through the lens of alignment.

Family responsibility continues to hold an important place while personal identity remains balanced and grounded.

Care and ambition operate within healthy boundaries.

The journaling moment signals internal readiness. Desire emerges from clarity and self-understanding.

When identity stabilizes, meaningful connection appears naturally.

Leadership now expresses itself as integrated presence.

Key Takeaways

1. Leadership matures as influence is exercised with composure and clarity.

2. Discernment guides opportunity toward sustainable direction.

3. When identity is coherent, both work and relationships grow from stability and authenticity.

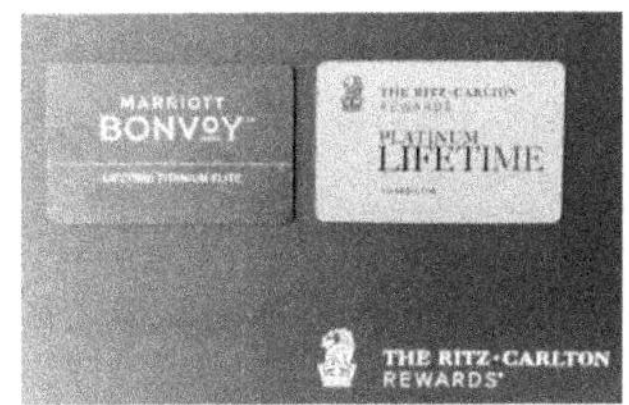

Q34

It sounds like that connection came at a meaningful moment in your life. How did she impact you and what began to shift for you because of that relationship?

Meeting her felt immediate and natural. From the beginning, there was an ease between us—a sense that we could talk endlessly and effortlessly. We shared long nights of conversation about life, work, travel, music, films, and ideas. She had a global sensibility shaped by her work in the fashion industry and her upbringing in Canada, and that perspective intrigued me. She understood my consulting work, respected the responsibility I carried, and was genuinely supportive of what I was building. Our connection deepened quickly. Within a few months, we decided to move together into a new condominium just down the street.

At the same time, something deeply meaningful unfolded: my mother moved into my girlfriend's apartment, which she was giving up. My mother had always dreamed of living in New York City, and for a period of about six months, that dream became reality. Having her close allowed us to spend real time together—walking through Central Park, talking, sharing meals—moments that felt grounded and complete.

During those walks through Central Park, she began sharing more stories from her younger years—especially about Milan, Italy. My mother had been born in the small mountain village of Castroregio in Calabria, a place with only a few dozen residents. As a young woman, her world expanded when she moved north to Milan, where she worked in the fashion industry as a seamstress and studied mathematics in evening classes despite having little formal schooling. She loved Milan—the elegance of the city, the rhythm of its streets, and the creativity of the fashion houses. Even after our family later moved south to Taranto, she often spoke about those years with a quiet affection, and she retained a graceful Milanese way of speaking that my brother sometimes teased her about, though I always admired it. Walking with her through New York, I could see that same spark. In many ways the city reminded her of Milan—alive, stylish, full of possibility. Those conversations helped me understand where her sense of grace and hospitality came from, and how deeply those qualities had influenced me.

As life stabilized, my girlfriend and I began traveling extensively together. Travel had always been important to me, but now it became a shared experience—and a laboratory for observation. I introduced her to the Marriott family of hotels, particularly The Ritz-Carlton, a brand whose philosophy resonated deeply with me. My connection to Marriott went back years. It was the first hotel brand I stayed with after college, and I had even met Bill Marriott early in my career. His leadership philosophy, *Spirit to Serve*, left a lasting impression on me. Long before I ever consulted formally in hospitality, I was offering thoughtful, constructive feedback— often through the small red comment cards Marriott placed in guest rooms. It was an expression of care. I was instinctively looking at service, efficiency, flow, and human experience—shaped by my upbringing, my professional discipline, and my belief that excellence is lived, not imposed. That instinct only deepened when I experienced The Ritz-Carlton. Their Gold Standards felt aligned with something I had been articulating internally for years.

During our stays, I engaged thoughtfully with general managers and, over time, with senior leaders—including Simon Cooper, then President and Chief Operating Officer of The Ritz-Carlton Hotel Company, and Bob Kharazmi, Executive Vice President of Global Operations at the time. Our interactions were rooted in mutual respect. I shared observations; they listened. What I consistently emphasized was the importance of warmth and graciousness—moving beyond formality toward making guests feel genuinely at "home." That sensibility resonated, and over time, it became increasingly visible in how the brand expressed its service philosophy. What stood out to me was that service excellence, when paired with humility and openness, creates trust at every level. My girlfriend witnessed all of this. She saw how my philosophy expressed itself naturally—lived in practice and embodied as a way of being.

During that period, subtle friction began to surface between us. Our lives were moving with different rhythms. I was deepening my inner work, clarifying my leadership philosophy, and integrating purpose with execution, while she was navigating her own professional direction. When she received an offer for a senior role with a fashion company in Los Angeles, the opportunity felt like a moment worth embracing together. I believed a change of environment and a fresh chapter might strengthen our relationship while also reopening creative possibilities that had first drawn me to Los

Angeles. With my mother now settled back in New Jersey and reconnecting with my brother, the timing felt supportive of the move.

We decided to return to Los Angeles together and see where the next chapter might lead.

Reflections

This scene reveals leadership expressed through relationship and environment rather than hierarchy.

What stands out is the integration of philosophy into lived experience.

Service excellence becomes embodied—observed in hotels, refined through dialogue, and expressed through thoughtful engagement with leaders. Influence operates through presence and credibility rather than position.

The time spent with his mother in New York adds another quiet layer of influence.

Her memories of Milan—its elegance, craftsmanship, and cosmopolitan spirit—reveal where some of his own appreciation for grace, hospitality, and metropolitan life first took root.

Leadership, like culture, is often inherited through observation long before it is articulated.

The connection with his girlfriend becomes both mirror and catalyst.

Shared travel and conversation allow values to be explored in motion.

Leadership expresses itself through everyday interactions—how space is entered, feedback is offered, and warmth and graciousness shape the experience of others.

The emerging friction carries its own lesson. Alignment deepens through awareness of differences in rhythm and direction. Growth reveals how individuals evolve at their own pace.

Key Takeaways

1. Leadership becomes visible through everyday interactions when philosophy is lived with consistency and presence.

2. Service excellence practiced with humility builds trust and influence across every environment.

3. Relationships illuminate alignment by revealing differences in rhythm, direction, and personal evolution.

Q35

After returning to Los Angeles, how did you adapt to that transition and what began to take shape as a result?

At the same time we relocated to Los Angeles, another seed—one that had been quietly forming for years—began to surface more clearly.

For some time, I had been applying the COS philosophy—Creative Optimum Self—in my consulting work and in my life. I was sharing the principles with clients, colleagues, and individuals who sought guidance. I facilitated conversations, small workshops, and even pro bono engagements, including speaking at organizations such as the Glendale YWCA. The feedback was consistent: what I was articulating helped people see themselves and their work more clearly.

My girlfriend saw that before I fully did. She kept saying, simply and insistently, "You should write this down. This should be a book." Her encouragement stayed with me. Just before leaving New York, I attended a conference in Puerto Rico called *The Alliance of a New Humanity*, led by Deepak Chopra. I had long admired his writing and his journey—how he bridged consciousness and leadership—and I appreciated the way he brought spiritual inquiry into mainstream dialogue. Meeting him personally was meaningful. It reinforced that these conversations belonged in the world. Combined with my girlfriend's steady encouragement, something crystallized. I knew it was time to write. For three weeks, I wrote almost nonstop—often eight hours a day. The ideas were already clear in my mind and in my practice. Writing simply allowed them to move from lived experience onto the page.

When we later settled in Glendale, California, I completed and refined the manuscript there. The book was titled: *The Way: Live Your Dream, It's Not a Secret!,* now evolved into *Creative Optimum Self, Transform Your Life and Your World.* The structure was intentional—intimate in tone, personal and direct, and carefully architected. It offered five Inner Steps and five Outer Steps based on my practice philosophy, *Creative Optimum Self.* Unlike many inspirational books that emphasized vision alone, this was a guide. It bridged inner clarity with disciplined execution.

Through a personal connection, I sent the manuscript to Leonard Riggio, then CEO of Barnes & Noble, who forwarded it to Edward Ash-Milby, the buyer responsible for inspirational titles at the time. Edward read it and responded with clarity: he felt the book was strong, timely, and grounded—arriving at a moment when many were seeking meaning yet lacked structure. His advice was direct: publish it independently through my company, and Barnes & Noble would purchase it. That is exactly what I did. Within months, *The Way: Live Your Dream, It's Not a Secret!* was available through Barnes & Noble and Amazon. I participated in events in both New York and Los Angeles—something that had begun as private writing in New York only months earlier. What had once lived internally as philosophy had now become a public expression.

At the same time, life was unfolding personally. My girlfriend had begun her role in Los Angeles, and her work visa was nearing expiration. We were already living as partners. Marriage felt aligned—steady, intentional, and grounded in shared transition. Creation and commitment unfolded together.

Reflections

This scene marks authorship.

The writing emerges from integration. The ideas have already been tested across consulting engagements, caregiving, collapse, renewal, and leadership. Language simply gives structure to what has been lived.

The buyer's response affirms something essential: inspiration thrives when it is supported by structure, and structure becomes meaningful when it carries humanity. The work brings those two dimensions together.

Marriage and authorship unfold in parallel—commitment in life and commitment in philosophy reinforcing one another.

The Creative Optimum Self moves from lived embodiment into articulated framework.

Private clarity becomes public offering.

Key Takeaways

1. When lived philosophy matures, articulation becomes natural expression.

2. Structure allows inspiration to move into practical application.

3. Authorship begins when personal integration becomes service to others.

CHAPTER SIX

When Strength Becomes the Weight

Achievement, Absorption, and the Point of Saturation

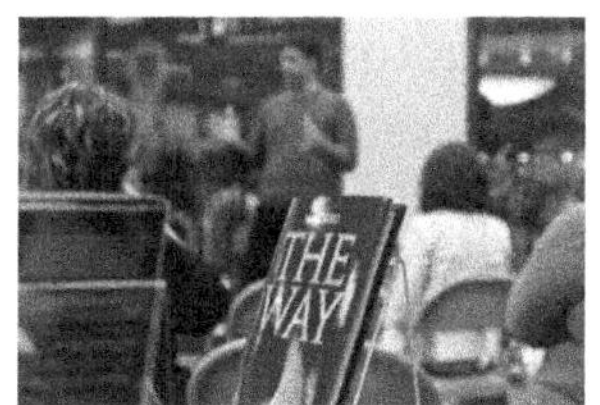

Q36

That season moved quickly—writing, publishing, touring, and getting married.

How did that period unfold for you?

That season moved quickly—fast-paced, intense—and in the middle of writing, editing, producing, publishing, and preparing for the book tour, we did get married.

We had a private ceremony in our home. My mother had planned to visit, and the timing aligned beautifully as we prepared baked manicotti Milanese-style together. We invited our neighbors, a few friends we had made since relocating and members of the Barnes & Noble team supporting my book. It was intimate and quiet. Looking back now, I can see there were unresolved tensions between us. I had acknowledged them privately before the marriage. In hindsight, a slower pace may have created more space for clarity. Yet the season was moving quickly—creatively and emotionally—and I chose to move with it. She had encouraged the book from the beginning and believed in what I was building. Her support was steady, even if limited in capacity. As often happened in my life, I carried the greater share of the responsibility.

The book tour itself, however, was incredibly affirming. The first stop was in Princeton NJ, my home area. About twenty-five people attended, which is a strong turnout for a first-time, unknown author. I spoke about the book, shared its origins, and explained the philosophy behind it. People were engaged, asking thoughtful questions. I noticed a man sitting in the back—wearing a suit, arms folded, nodding quietly with a steady smile. I couldn't tell whether he was deeply aligned or preparing to challenge me.

At the end of the event, he approached me and said, "Thank you. I'm going to buy a dozen copies of your book." He explained that he had been speaking to his staff for years about this exact idea—the inner wisdom we all carry—and that the way I articulated Creative Optimum Self resonated deeply with him. That gentleman was Craig Lafferty, the CEO of United Way of Mercer County. We stayed in touch over the years until his passing. That moment crystallized everything for me. In that moment I felt confirmed in releasing the message of *The Way*.

I printed 2,500 hardcover copies—not a bestseller by any commercial measure—and I still have a few copies today. But the impact mattered far more than the numbers. That was why I wrote the book: to share something lived and real—a way of being that had helped me survive, grow, and could serve to inspire others.

Reflections

This scene captures a period of acceleration.

Creation, commitment, and public visibility converge within a narrow window of time. A philosophy moves from private manuscript to printed form while a marriage is formalized in the same season. The ceremony is intimate. The tour is affirming. The rooms are full enough to matter.

Momentum carries both confidence and quiet tension. The book enters the world with resonance. Recognition arrives through individuals rather than scale. Beneath the forward motion, unspoken questions remain present—recorded quietly in journals yet set aside as life continues to move forward.

The scene closes at a peak: productive, visible, and still unfolding.

Key Takeaways

1. Velocity magnifies structure. When life accelerates, both strengths and unresolved tensions intensify simultaneously.

2. Awareness reaches its full power when accompanied by integration.

3. Impact is established through resonance before recognition. Depth of connection precedes scale.

Q37

After the book tour and getting married, how did life begin to unfold—both in your work and in your relationship?

On the surface, life appeared full and expansive—the book had been published, the tour was underway, and opportunities to speak and share the philosophy were growing. The book became a living extension of my work.

During this time, I was invited to speak on radio programs and to facilitate workshops with nonprofit organizations, including the YWCA, speaking to counselors who work directly with battered women—professionals who carry the emotional weight of trauma. The focus was on how they might maintain inner balance while serving others in deeply painful circumstances.

I was also invited to speak with high school girls at a local school in Glendale. Those conversations were especially meaningful. Many of them were just beginning to shape their sense of identity and direction, and I shared with them the importance of learning early how to care for themselves— how inner practices such as reflection, discipline, and self-respect can guide life choices before outside pressures begin to define them. Speaking with both the counselors and the young women reinforced something important to me: the philosophy was meant to support people at every stage of life.

One moment during the workshop with the YWCA counselors struck me unexpectedly. When I entered the room, I noticed a drawing on the whiteboard—a small boy surrounded by pockets of tension all around him. The presenter explained that domestic violence does not only impact women; it profoundly affects children, especially boys who witness it and are forced to participate in it. I felt a physical reaction—a stillness, followed by a wave of recognition. In that moment, something surfaced that I had never fully allowed myself to see: I was that child who had experienced emotional and internal abuse. Until then, I had long believed that I had emerged largely untouched by it—resilient, responsible, self-sufficient. Seeing that image revealed something deeper. It was the first time I consciously recognized how profoundly my childhood environment had shaped my internal wiring.

Around that same period, I was invited to speak at several community and professional events, including one hosted by the Southern California Book Publicists Group, where I received a humanitarian award recognizing the time and care I had been donating to community workshops and outreach. I spoke about the book, about service, responsibility, and the quiet obligation that arises when our work begins to reach others.

At the same time, new layers were emerging in my marriage. There were moments of emotional volatility that I hadn't fully understood at first. Over time, I began to notice that these outbursts often coincided with alcohol. I later learned that her father had struggled with alcoholism—something I hadn't known before—and that awareness helped contextualize what I was witnessing. One night the situation escalated to a point where I feared for both our safety. I made the difficult decision to call the police—not out of anger, but out of responsibility. I loved her, and we had just been married. My instinct, shaped by years of caregiving and leadership, was to stabilize and help wherever I could.

Meanwhile, the message of the book was continuing to resonate in the outside world. Reviews began appearing, and one in particular stayed with me. Written by a veteran reporter, it observed that while many of the principles explored in *The Way* had existed across generations, what mattered was the clarity with which they were expressed—and that the book could support those who were ready and open to receive it. That sentence stayed with me. It reaffirmed why I had written the book. I wasn't theorizing—I was living these principles. They had helped me survive, grow, and serve others.

At times, I quietly wished the same principles could reach even closer to home. The philosophy that was helping others find clarity and stability was the same philosophy I hoped might guide our own relationship. In many ways, that hope stayed with me as I continued moving forward.

Reflections

This scene expands the narrative in two directions at once.

Publicly, the philosophy begins to circulate.

The work moves outward into communities, classrooms, and organizations where people are searching for clarity and strength.

Privately, a deeper realization emerges. In a room dedicated to understanding trauma, a simple drawing becomes a mirror. The recognition is immediate and physical.

The resilient child who carried responsibility for so long becomes visible in a new way. What once appeared as strength alone reveals its deeper origins in survival.

At the same time, instability begins to surface within the marriage, while affirmation continues in the public world.

The instinct to stabilize and protect remains active, shaped by a lifetime of responsibility and care.

The philosophy is being lived in real time—through service, memory, relationship, and awareness, as deeper understanding comes into view.

Key Takeaways

1. Leadership maturity includes the ability to witness personal history as it surfaces, without abandoning responsibility in the present.

2. External recognition can coincide with internal revelation. Growth in one domain does not pause evolution in another.

3. Strength that stabilizes others must eventually turn inward. Awareness is the first signal that deeper integration is required.

Q38

Now that the book was published, what shifted for you professionally and personally?

On the business front, I felt a deep sense of peace. I had been living and applying these principles for over a decade, and publishing the book brought a feeling of completion. The philosophy was no longer only lived—it was articulated, tested, and now visible in the world. What became clear to me was how universal the principles truly were. I had applied them successfully across industries—media, entertainment, banking, insurance—and during this period I was also consulting in healthcare with Kaiser Permanente, supporting large-scale programs and program management initiatives. Alongside that work, I continued facilitating workshops, which allowed me to see the philosophy operate both as a personal framework and as a practical leadership system.

Around the same time, I reached another important milestone: I formally registered the trademarks. **Creative Optimum Self, Creative Optimum Solutions, and COS** were all approved—anchoring both the inner philosophy and its application in the business world. From a legacy standpoint, the work now carried structure, identity, and continuity.

On a personal level, life was becoming more complex. Shortly after the book's release, my wife lost her job. The loss affected her deeply. Discouragement gradually deepened into depression, and the emotional volatility at home intensified. I found myself trying to understand what I was witnessing—whether it was the impact of losing her work, the strain of transition, or something deeper unfolding between us. My instinct, as it often had been throughout my life, was to support and stabilize. I helped her search for new opportunities, encouraged her to focus on her health, and supported her decision to pursue physical training and fitness as a path back toward balance. In many ways I became both emotional anchor and practical guide—offering presence, patience, and encouragement during a vulnerable period.

At the same time, I observed something quietly unsettling. I had written the book to share a way of living—an invitation rather than instruction. Yet I could see that while she respected the philosophy, applying it in her own life remained challenging. I held the principles with conviction while also witnessing someone I loved struggle outside of them.

When a consulting opportunity emerged in San Francisco with First Republic Bank, the timing felt meaningful on several levels. Professionally, it aligned well with my experience and values. Personally, it offered a different kind of reset. Rather than relocating immediately, I structured the engagement so that I could commute. We moved into a beautiful place in Glendale, and I began traveling to San Francisco during the week—typically staying three or four days at a time—returning home on weekends. That rhythm created space to breathe. The physical distance softened the intensity between us. Seeing each other less frequently allowed tension to settle, conversations to unfold more calmly, and daily friction to ease. For nearly a year this arrangement worked. She continued building her work in fitness, and I remained deeply engaged in my consulting engagements, traveling back and forth while holding both worlds with intention.

When the contract eventually concluded and our lease came to an end, the tone of our relationship felt different—lighter and more hopeful. We agreed to try living in San Francisco together, trusting that the new environment might help sustain the balance we had been cultivating.

Reflections

This scene illustrates integration under simultaneous pressure.

Professionally, momentum expands. The philosophy gains structure. Trademarks are secured.

Enterprise engagements deepen. The external architecture of the work grows stronger and more defined.

At home, emotional turbulence begins to surface. The environment calls for steadiness, patience, and careful observation.

What becomes visible here is bandwidth. The same systems used to guide large-scale transformation programs begins to shape personal life as well—adjusting structure, creating space, and recalibrating rhythm.

Distance functions as an intentional adjustment within the system. Space allows emotional pressure to settle and restores equilibrium.

Leadership in this moment expresses itself through containment—the ability to hold professional expansion and personal fragility at the same time while remaining centered and composed.

Key Takeaways

1. Integrated leadership operates across domains. The steadiness required to guide complex organizations also supports clarity in personal life.

2. Strategic space can strengthen relationships. Adjusting structure, cadence, and proximity often restores balance and perspective.

3. Containment is a leadership discipline. Holding expansion and fragility simultaneously requires bandwidth, restraint, and composure.

Q39

Sometimes a change in environment can bring renewed balance—or simply create space to see things more clearly.

Did the move to San Francisco strengthen your relationship with your wife in any meaningful way?

For a time, the move to San Francisco did bring a sense of stability. We settled into a beautiful condominium overlooking the water—calm, light-filled, and grounding. For the first few months, we explored the area together, traveled nearby, and enjoyed the novelty of a new chapter. We spent weekends at places we loved, including The Ritz-Carlton at Half Moon Bay, which became a familiar retreat for us. Her parents came to visit and stayed with us for a week. Her brother joined as well. Hosting them, showing them the city, and sharing our life together felt meaningful. It gave the sense that our relationship was finding its footing.

Professionally, things were also aligning well. I secured a senior consulting engagement with Pacific Gas and Electric, working on a large-scale smart meter initiative. The office was a short walk from where we lived, and the work itself was substantial, long-term, and deeply aligned with my experience in systems transformation and leadership. The initiative involved coordinating and managing Accenture consulting resources—an environment I was comfortable navigating, given my prior experience working alongside teams from Deloitte and PricewaterhouseCoopers in earlier enterprise engagements. That background made it natural for me to align large advisory groups within complex programs. I continued facilitating workshops alongside the consulting work, integrating the philosophy into both practice and presence.

During this period, she found a sales position with Tiffany & Co. in San Francisco. It was a welcome shift—less pressure than the director-level roles she had held before, and something she genuinely enjoyed. With reduced stress, her energy felt lighter. We began forming friendships in our building, reconnecting socially, and establishing a more regular rhythm together. Looking back, that year in San Francisco was one of relative calm.

When she was later offered a director position with Tiffany in Santa Monica—leading the opening of a new store—it felt like another step forward. I supported the opportunity fully. Although it meant returning to commuting, I was open to moving back to Southern California, which I had always felt more connected to. We secured a condominium in Malibu overlooking the water. The view stretched wide across the Pacific, light shifting throughout the day, the horizon wide and uninterrupted. In the mornings, we would often stand on the balcony and watch dolphins swim past—surfacing in rhythm, gliding through the waves, occasionally leaping in arcs that felt almost choreographed. It was peaceful, expansive, and beautiful in a way that invited hope. She focused on launching the new store. From my perspective, things were stabilizing again. There was progress, momentum, and—for the first time in a long while—a quiet sense that we might be ready to start a family. It had always been something I envisioned for my life. I had carried that desire quietly through every chapter, even during seasons of uncertainty. We had been through a great deal, and I felt we might finally be ready to build a family together.

Reflections

This scene reflects a period of stability taking shape.

Environment, work, and relationship begin to align, creating a rhythm that feels steady and sustainable.

Shared experiences—travel, hosting family, daily routines—restore a sense of connection and normalcy.

What becomes visible is the effect of consistency over time. Stability is not assumed; it is built through presence, structure, and continued effort.

Key Takeaways

1. Leadership includes environmental design. Where you live, how you structure time, and how you regulate pressure directly affect relational stability.

2. Stability is often built through rhythm rather than intensity. Clear roles, shared routines, and reduced volatility allow strength to reconstitute.

3. Supporting another person's growth requires steadiness, not control. Leadership in personal life is expressed through patience, structure, and consistency.

Q40

After returning to Southern California and settling into a new rhythm—with your wife stepping into a major leadership role and you continuing to commute for work—

how did that transition unfold personally and emotionally?

When we returned to Southern California, on the surface, things appeared promising. We settled into a beautiful place in Malibu overlooking the ocean. My wife stepped into a significant leadership role—opening a new Tiffany store in Santa Monica. She was capable, driven, and deeply invested in the responsibility. I was genuinely proud of her. It felt like an important milestone, and I hoped it would bring her a sense of fulfillment and grounding. Professionally, my work continued to expand. I remained engaged with Pacific Gas and Electric in San Francisco, commuting back and forth, while staying grounded in the practices that had long sustained me.

At first, the structure helped. The distance created space, and the routine felt manageable. But slowly, something began to feel off. This time, the distance didn't create clarity—it created absence. My wife became less responsive. Calls went unanswered. Messages were delayed or ignored. When I tried to talk about it, I sensed deflection rather than openness. There was a familiar pattern emerging—one I had seen before—where difficult conversations were avoided rather than addressed.

Around that same period, something else unsettled me. One weekend we attended the Screen Actors Guild Awards, an event I had been fortunate to attend several times over the years through my membership in the Screen Actors Guild. When we returned home, we discovered that our house had been broken into while we were away. A number of personal belongings were taken. At first, we suspected it may have been someone with access to the property. We couldn't prove anything, but the violation lingered.

A month later, after installing a security system, the alarm sounded in the middle of the night. It was close to two in the morning. I woke up to the sound and saw a man running down the exterior steps outside our home. The police were called. No one was apprehended. Nothing further happened. Yet something in me shifted. I found myself quietly questioning whether the existence of a life insurance policy—where she was listed as the primary beneficiary—meant anything in the context of what had happened. I could not explain the thought fully, and I never confronted her with any accusation. But a subtle layer of distrust entered my body. Safety, which I had always assumed, no longer felt automatic. I carried that feeling quietly.

As this unfolded, memories I had once pushed aside resurfaced. I remembered a trip years earlier to Canada, visiting friends from her past. One evening, while we were all together, a man—a married friend—crossed a boundary and became physically inappropriate with her in front of both me and his wife. I remember the discomfort, the confusion, the internal alarm. Later that same weekend, other moments followed—subtle, unsettling—that I had rationalized at the time in order to keep the peace. Now, with distance and silence replacing connection, those memories returned—not as accusations, but as signals I had ignored. I noticed another shift as well: I was always the one traveling to see her. She no longer came to visit me. Emotional availability gave way to emotional distance. The more responsibility she took on at work, the more guarded and inaccessible she became at home.

I turned inward. I revisited my journals—years of reflections documenting cycles of tension, reconciliation, and repair. I saw a pattern clearly now: again and again, I had assumed the role of caretaker, mediator, therapist. I had learned how to restore peace—but often at the cost of my own well-being. This time, something in me resisted returning to that role. I felt depleted, suffocated, and off balance. I was carrying the relationship, my work, my vision, and my health—and the imbalance was no longer sustainable. The weight began to show physically and emotionally.

Around this time, my mother expressed a desire to return to Italy. It had been many years since she had gone back. I invited my wife to come with us—hoping, perhaps, that sharing my roots and my history might reconnect us. She declined. Work came first—I was not surprised. What I didn't yet know was that this decision—this trip back to Italy—would quietly become a turning point.

For the first time in a long while, I felt myself listening differently—not to hope, not to obligation, but to truth.

This scene carries accumulation.

The structure that once stabilized now exposes distance. Work expands. Responsibility increases. Communication thins.

Silence begins to replace rhythm. Signals resurface. What was once rationalized returns as pattern.

The role of caretaker becomes heavier. Repair requires more energy. Reciprocity diminishes.

The shift unfolds quietly within. Bandwidth narrows. The body begins to register the cost.

An invitation to return to Italy appears—not as escape, but as origin. The listening changes. Hope softens. Obligation loosens. The weight is no longer abstract. It is deeply personal.

Key Takeaways

1. Space reveals structure. When rhythm changes, patterns become visible without confrontation.

2. Leadership in personal life requires reciprocity. Sustained responsibility without mutual engagement narrows capacity.

3. Alignment across domains matters. Professional expansion cannot absorb unresolved emotional imbalance indefinitely.

Q41

What did returning to Italy with your mother mean to you at that point in your life?

The trip to Italy came at exactly the right moment. In many ways, it felt guided by something greater than circumstance.

Years earlier, I had taken my mother on a long trip across the United States. We traveled first class, spent time together in Chicago, Las Vegas, and California, and she often shared that those weeks were among the happiest of her life. But there was one journey we had never taken together: returning to Italy—the country she left behind for me to have a better future. That absence had lived quietly inside me for decades. Ever since we immigrated, I had carried a deep, unresolved question: *Why did we leave?*

Italy was not just a place I was born—it was a place I loved. Leaving it had created a void I never fully understood until I returned. Being back—walking the streets, reconnecting with cousins who had helped raise me, standing in the kitchens and rooms I remembered vividly from childhood—was profoundly grounding. I could recall details from when I was six or seven years old as if no time had passed. My mother took me to where she was born, raised, and where our family history lived—including the resting place of my grandmother.

We spent three weeks in Paola, in Calabria—the same region where my mother was born—with my mom's niece Nina, who had been a constant presence in my childhood. Although she was my mother's niece, they were the same age, and she helped raise me when I was a little boy before we left for America. Seeing her again brought back a deep sense of familiarity and affection. During that visit she was already battling cancer, and although she had two sisters and a daughter of her own, she asked to stay primarily with my mother and me during those weeks. We spent long hours together talking, remembering, and simply being present with one another. A few months later she passed away. Being there with her during that time—holding her hand and sharing those final weeks—became one of the most meaningful parts of the trip.

In the meantime, something fundamental shifted in me. I felt restored and *reintegrated*—the joy, warmth, and belonging I experienced reconnected me to a part of myself that had been dormant for years. The strength that returned was calm, certain, and embodied. During that time, my relationship with my wife faded almost entirely into the background. Not out of avoidance—but because clarity had finally arrived. I could feel the difference unmistakably—one state narrowing, the other expanding. One heavy, the other alive. By the time I was ready to return to the United States, I knew what I had to do.

At the airport, my wife picked me up. My mother stayed behind in Italy. As we drove home, she told me she was ready to have a child together. And I knew, with complete certainty, that I was ready to end the marriage. The trip did not break me—it *strengthened* me. It gave me the courage to choose truth over fear, clarity over endurance, and life over survival.

Reflections

This scene returns to origin. Geography becomes grounding. Memory becomes present. Identity reconnects with environment.

Rooms once left behind are entered again. Voices from childhood reappear. The body remembers what the mind had adapted away.

The shift is internal and steady. Reintegration replaces fragmentation. Strength returns without urgency.

With distance came clarity. The emotional noise that once surrounded the relationship gradually softened, allowing a quiet but unmistakable understanding to emerge. The decision formed with calm certainty rather than conflict.

Key Takeaways

1. Leadership deepens when identity is reintegrated. Decisions grounded in origin carry steadiness rather than reaction.

2. Strength matures into discernment. The clearest turning points often arrive as calm certainty.

3. Self-leadership requires authorship. Choosing alignment over endurance marks the transition from survival to sovereignty.

Q42

Once you returned from Italy with clarity about what you needed to do, how did your wife respond?

When I returned, I was calm, clear, and resolved. I had found my center again, and I knew I would end the marriage. My wife's response was not confrontation or grief, but indifference. In retrospect, I believe she assumed I would not follow through. In the past, I had raised concerns and spoken about the possibility of separation if things did not change—and she had come to rely on my loyalty, patience, capacity to carry weight far beyond what was sustainable. What struck me most was not what she said, but what she did not offer.

Around that time, I went for a routine eye exam. The optometrist noticed an abnormality and referred me urgently to UCLA for further testing. I was frightened—the word *oncology* was mentioned, and the uncertainty alone was overwhelming. When I shared this with her, seeking reassurance or comfort, her response was not concern for my health, but anxiety about what it might mean for her own stability. That moment clarified everything.

We separated shortly after. I moved out quietly, leaving most of what we had built behind. I took a temporary residence at The Ritz-Carlton in downtown Los Angeles, as my work continued to accelerate. I had taken on a senior engagement role with AT&T during a major transition, and professionally I remained steady—even as my personal life was dismantling. I filed for divorce. The process unfolded slowly, over the course of nearly a year. During that time, I was traveling frequently between Los Angeles and Italy, where I had made a personal investment in restoring a family home with a distant cousin—a place I believed would represent continuity, healing, and return.

At the same time, my mother's health began to decline. After a fall in Italy and a period of rehabilitation, it became clear that she did not want to remain there permanently, despite being surrounded by family. The past carried too much unresolved pain for her. She wanted to be near me. Once again, I adjusted. As the divorce approached finalization, I prepared to return with her to California. I secured a new home in Marina del Rey—close to the ocean—with the intention of placing her nearby in assisted living, where I could remain present and supportive. The day we moved into that home was the same day the divorce was finalized. It felt like closure—quiet, legal, irreversible. I believed I was finally free to rebuild with integrity and intention.

I did not yet realize how much weight still remained.

Reflections

This scene marks decisive reorganization.

Clarity is no longer internal—it becomes action. The separation unfolds without spectacle. No collapse. Only movement aligned with truth.

The absence of reciprocity becomes visible not through argument, but through response to vulnerability. Health uncertainty exposes emotional asymmetry.

Simultaneously, external responsibility expands. Senior work continues. Family obligation increases. Legal dissolution proceeds. Leadership is expressed through containment rather than performance.

Multiple life structures dissolve and are rebuilt at once—marriage, home, geography, parental care—without fragmentation.

Key Takeaways

1. Leadership matures when clarity becomes action. Acting on what you already know restores alignment and prevents prolonged misdirection.

2. Emotional reciprocity is a structural requirement in both partnership and leadership. Commitment without mutuality eventually destabilizes the system.

3. Stability under simultaneous transitions reveals internal architecture. When identity remains intact amid dissolution, resilience has become embodied.

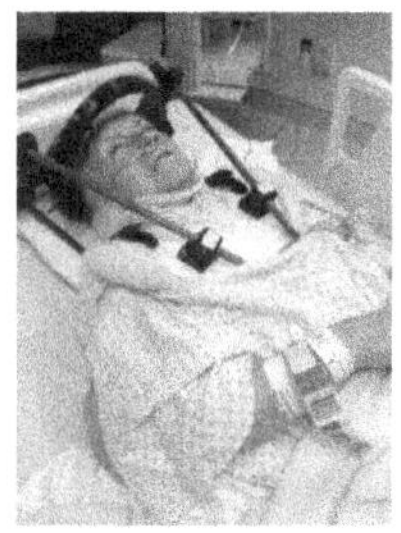

Q43

As you stepped into full responsibility for your mother's care while continuing to lead complex work engagements, how did that season of your life unfold?

What followed was an accumulation of events—pressure gathered from every direction at once. After my divorce was finalized, my mother came to live with me. I had also invited a distant cousin to stay temporarily while we finalized plans for a shared family home in Italy. She had recently lost her mother Nina, my mother's niece, and grief was still raw. Over time, her emotional instability began to surface in ways that affected my mother directly. I realized quickly that this arrangement was not healthy or safe for either of us, and I made the difficult decision to end that plan and help her return home.

At the same time, I was leading a major transformation initiative with DirecTV—a complex, high-stakes program involving infrastructure, billing, and operational systems. I was carrying professional responsibility during the day while reviewing the best long term living arrangement for my mom. Then one evening, everything changed. I had stepped outside briefly to clear my head when I heard a scream inside the condo—a large scream I will never forget. My mother had fallen. She was using a walker and had collapsed near the bedroom doorway. I rushed to her, instinctively cradling her head and neck, afraid she had broken her neck. I called 911 with one hand while holding her completely still with the other. The paramedics were careful to move her gently. She was first taken to a nearby hospital and then transferred to UCLA's trauma center. There, a team of medical professionals surrounded her immediately. The diagnosis was a C2 fracture—a life-threatening injury.

The doctors later shared with me that how I held her likely saved her life. They fitted her with a metal halo—an eight-pound structure secured to her skull to immobilize her neck. She would live with it for three months. I was present for every step—helping doctors, managing her care, taking her to therapy, cleaning her wounds, and making sure she was never alone. All of this was happening while I continued consulting—sleeping only a few hours a night, managing my responsibilities, and navigating growing professional friction as my guidance on the DirecTV program was increasingly dismissed. Eventually, we mutually agreed to part ways. Around that same time, I received a formal legal notice from a brand I deeply respected—one I had trusted and supported for years—regarding an internal issue that felt misdirected and unresolved. Rather than clarity or accountability, it reflected deflection. That moment was quietly devastating. By then, every pillar I relied on had fractured:

My marriage was over,

My extended family ties had dissolved,

My brother was absent,

My work had stalled,

And I was carrying my mother's survival alone.

One night, after midnight, standing on the terrace of my condo building—nineteen floors high above the city—I felt something give way—deep exhaustion.

I remember thinking that if I disappeared, there was no one left who would truly notice.

For the first time in my life, I considered stepping beyond the terrace.

Reflections

This scene represents the moment when accumulated pressure reaches saturation. Caregiving intensifies while professional trust erodes, institutional respect weakens, and the stability of family relationships dissolves. The structures that once supported resilience gradually thin under the weight of sustained responsibility.

Externally, strength continues to function. Medical systems are coordinated, difficult decisions are made, and professional obligations are carried forward with discipline and composure. Yet internally, the reinforcement that once sustained that strength begins to disappear. Sleep shortens, vigilance increases, and isolation deepens as the emotional load grows heavier.

The moment on the terrace does not arise from impulse. It emerges from prolonged depletion registering in the body and nervous system after years of carrying responsibility without shared support. When endurance extends beyond the limits of human capacity, even the strongest structures begin to signal that something deeper must change.

Key Takeaways

1. Collapse rarely announces itself through drama. It accumulates through sustained responsibility carried without reinforcement.

2. High-functioning leadership can mask internal depletion. Competence under pressure does not replace relational support.

3. Strength without shared support becomes isolation. Mature leadership requires knowing when endurance has reached its limit.

CHAPTER SEVEN

Becoming the Witness

Integration, Continuity, and Constant Choices

Q44

After everything collapsed—your marriage, work and support system—you were standing at the edge, questioning whether anyone would even notice if you were gone.

What happened in that moment?

I believed I might jump.

Not out of rage or panic—but out of exhaustion.

That night, after midnight, I was sitting alone on the terrace. Everything had collapsed at once: my marriage, my work, my sense of belonging, even the institutions and people I once trusted. I was exhausted beyond words. I remember thinking, very clearly, *Who would even miss me?*

And then something familiar surfaced—my living practice. I remembered an exercise I had written about years earlier in *The Way*: stepping outside of yourself and observing your life as if you were watching a film. I had done this my entire life through journaling, often without realizing how powerful it was. In that moment, I began to watch my own story unfold. I saw myself as the central character moving through scenes—

childhood, loss, ambition, love, failure, responsibility. I noticed something striking: no matter how chaotic or painful the circumstances—I was always present.

I had a body that carried me through adversity. A mind that integrated emotion, logic, and intuition. Relationships—close and distant—that shaped me. And through it all, I had always transformed what was in front of me. I could see the pattern clearly: the precision of mathematics that taught me structure, the discipline of service that taught me responsibility, and the instinct for storytelling that shaped how I made meaning—together, they had always driven my ability to transform. That realization landed quietly and firmly: this is who I am—the one who navigates, integrates, and evolves through every circumstance and every collapse.

I decided to do the only thing I had ever done when life became unbearable—face what was directly in front of me. And what was in front of me was my mother. The next morning, I got up and followed the practice, prioritizing my day—I helped my mom out of bed, assisted her to the bathroom, cleaned and cared for her, fed her, and managed all her appointments. I learned how to be her physical therapist, emotional support, and advocate. I became her full-time caregiver.

In the process, I learned how the healthcare system truly works—when to question it, when to push back, and how to protect dignity through care. I turned down projects. For eighteen months, my entire world narrowed to caregiving. My mother was remarkable. Despite everything she had endured, she was disciplined, resilient, and determined. After three months, the halo was removed. Her neck healed cleanly. She completed eighteen months of treatment, regained strength, and learned to walk again with a walker. She was alive—and independent enough to move forward.

Eventually, we reached another decision point. The condominium I was leasing was being sold. I hadn't worked in a long time and was in debt. She encouraged me—firmly—to return to my life. I placed her in a beautiful, assisted living community overlooking the ocean in Santa Monica. And I moved into a small one-bedroom in the current building.

That was the turning point—a transformation grounded in awareness, emerging from a renewed connection with myself.

Reflections

This scene reveals the emergence of the witness during a period of profound compression.

In that moment, awareness rises beyond circumstance and observes identity with clarity.

The pattern becomes visible through compassion, love, and presence.

Caregiving becomes the stabilizing axis as ambition quiets, external validation recedes, and responsibility continues to guide daily action.

Integrated Being Intelligence becomes fully embodied, expressed through steady action and presence.

The collapse becomes a revealing moment, bringing forward the one who has always been navigating the journey.

Key Takeaways

1. Identity must be separated from circumstance. Leadership stabilizes when awareness becomes larger than events.

2. Witnessing transforms survival into agency. Observing one's own pattern restores authorship under pressure.

3. Integration expresses itself as the capacity to remain present, responsible, and grounded even when external structures fall away.

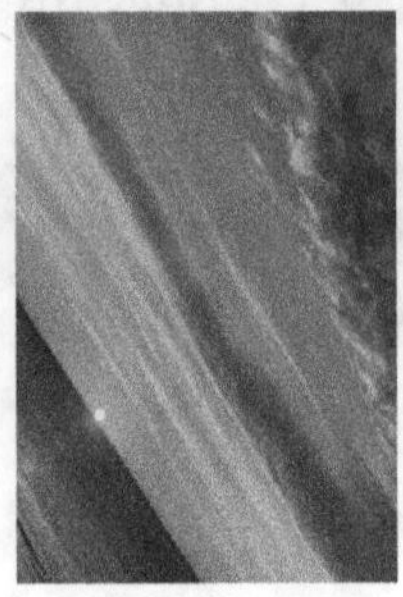

Q45

What changed in how you moved through life after that turning point?

What changed was subtle on the surface, yet decisive underneath.

On a personal level, I had been divorced for over two years and had not dated during that period. My focus had been on caregiving, integration, and rebuilding my internal foundation. Over time, something reopened. I met a few women who reminded me of my capacity for romance, curiosity, and connection. It was a return to aliveness. I realized I could love again. From that moment, I allowed myself to re-enter life fully and participate in it with presence.

Professionally, I moved with greater intentionality. I had closed my consulting company during the season of my divorce, bringing that chapter to completion. With a clearer sense of how my work had evolved, I re-established my practice—aligning Integrated Leadership Intelligence into my practice and holding it to a standard of excellence that reflected how I lived and led. The work that followed reflected that alignment. I secured a long-term engagement with Live Nation Entertainment and Ticketmaster, where responsibility expanded naturally as trust deepened. I was entrusted with more complex mandates and broader transformation initiatives. As my personal life became more grounded, my professional responsibilities expanded.

At home, responsibility intensified again. My mother experienced additional falls and transitions—assisted living, rehabilitation facilities, private caregiving arrangements—each revealing gaps in consistency and dignity. Drawing on everything I had learned, I made a decisive adjustment. I moved into a larger corner unit and brought her back into my home.

What followed became what I called a Ritz-Carlton-level nursing environment. I personally selected caregivers, trained them, rotated staff, coordinated nurses, and structured care around dignity, consistency, and respect. While leading enterprise transformations professionally, I was also operating a high-touch healthcare environment at home. It was demanding and aligned.

During this season, through a friend, I was introduced to Apple. She formed a deep bond with my mother immediately. Their connection brought warmth into a chapter that had required extraordinary endurance. It arrived as grace— steady, grounding, and unexpected. In that season, I noticed something steady within me. I moved through the world consciously—integrating life as it unfolded.

Reflections

This scene marks the transition from survival to authorship.

Stability is now intentional. Professional expansion resumes with maturity. Responsibility increases within coherence.

Caregiving intensifies with dignity preserved.

Authority expresses itself through steadiness. Decisions arise from integration.

Life remains complex, and alignment continues to guide movement.

Key Takeaways

1. Elevation follows integration. When internal coherence stabilizes, responsibility expands naturally and sustainably.

2. Mature leadership expresses itself in cadence, not force. Authority is demonstrated through steadiness and measured progression.

3. Excellence is contextual and consistent, expressed through the same standards that guide enterprise transformation, caregiving, partnership, and daily life.

Q46

What did daily life look like as caregiving and leadership began to coexist under the same roof?

Daily life became layered—intimate, demanding, and unexpectedly human. Apple had entered my life quietly, and just as quietly, she formed a deep bond with my mother. Having been raised by her grandparents, she carried a sensitivity toward elder care that felt instinctive. She didn't just help—she connected. At the same time, our relationship deepened naturally. What began as companionship became intimacy, and intimacy became shared living. Soon, the three of us were under the same roof—caring, building, and navigating life together. Then COVID arrived. The world contracted, and so did our external movement—but inside our home, something expanded.

For one year, we lived almost entirely within those walls—caregiving, companionship, and work unfolding simultaneously. What could have felt restrictive became presence. Apple supported my mother with warmth and patience, and in doing so created a relationship neither of us could have planned. It was a rare gift—time, closeness, and dignity—offered when the outside world had gone quiet.

As my mother's health declined, everything around her was handled with care. Hospice entered gently. Nothing felt rushed. Every detail was intentional. I would have kept her forever if love alone could have done it. When the priest came and witnessed the level of care, he told me I had done far more than most sons ever could. That stayed with me. My brother arrived days before she passed. They reconciled. There was peace. Apple and I promised my mother that we would remain a family—that what had formed between us would continue. When my mother took her final breath, her body grew still, but her face held a smile. Painful, yes—but unmistakably peaceful. She left whole.

In the weeks that followed, while I was still moving through quiet layers of grief, another loss arrived—this time from a different part of my life. On my birthday morning, Apple and I were staying at The Ritz-Carlton in Cancún when the news came that Arne Sorenson had passed away. I was stunned. Only weeks earlier, he had sent condolences for my mother. Over the years, our connection had grown from a documentary conversation into something genuine—rooted in shared values. He embodied leadership with dignity and humanity. Even during illness, his messages carried gratitude and grace. When I walk into a property today, I still see it through the lens of integrity he modeled.

After Apple traveled to Thailand to be with her family, she returned carrying a quiet urgency. Her grandmother, ninety years old, was nearing the end of her life. Apple shared that she was the remaining granddaughter who had not yet married, and she asked if we could be married so her grandmother could witness it. It did not feel like a crossroads. We were already a family. We were living together, caring together, grieving together. Saying yes was continuity.

We were married in a simple ceremony at Palisades Park in Santa Monica, a place woven into our shared rhythm. A few close friends stood beside us. We wrote our own vows. Apple's family watched from Thailand as we exchanged them. It was intimate, unforced, and deeply joyful. Apple was happy. Her grandmother was happy. And weeks later, her grandmother passed—having received that gift.

Life moved forward with quiet coherence.

Reflections

This chapter reflects leadership expressed through presence rather than force.

Caregiving, grief, partnership, and commitment unfold through steadiness.

Intimacy deepens alongside responsibility.

Loss becomes part of the refinement of identity, deepening presence and understanding.

Marriage emerges as a natural continuation of what had already been lived and shared.

Key Takeaways

1. Leadership matures when private responsibility equals public discipline. The most important authority is exercised in quiet rooms.

2. Alignment reduces unnecessary drama. When identity is integrated, major decisions feel natural and grounded.

3. Commitment grows strongest through shared presence. Stability allows love to be chosen with clarity.

Q47

How did marriage feel the second time around—and did the desire to build a family still live within you?

Yes—the desire to build a family never left. When I look back across my life, that longing stands out as the one thread that remained unresolved. The wish to share joy, experience, and wisdom with children of my own was always present, even when circumstances didn't allow it to take shape. When Apple and I married, it felt like that door might finally open. We spoke openly about it. It was part of our plan.

Then external pressures arrived. The war in Ukraine, rushed financial decisions, and poor investment advice led to a significant setback. At the same time, years of caregiving, accumulated stress, and the weight of COVID had taken a toll on my health. That period required recalibration. I refined my nutrition with intention—returning to a disciplined Mediterranean structure, calibrating not only what I ate but when I ate. I paid attention to rhythm, timing, and recovery. The physical transformation was visible. The deeper shift was responsiveness—listening carefully when the body speaks.

With that recalibration came clarity. I believed Apple would be in my life forever. I wanted her to truly know me—not just who I was in the present, but the full arc of where I came from. She was new to the United States and hadn't yet experienced much of it—we decided to travel together. I showed her the places where I grew up, studied, and where work had taken me. We traveled across the U.S., then to Europe—Italy, Paris, Switzerland—and later to Tokyo and Thailand, where she shared her world with me. It felt important that our lives weren't just shared forward, but understood backward. When we returned, we chose to begin again—intentionally. We donated our furniture, moved to Orange County, selected a new home together, and created a clean slate. The idea was simple: we were building something new, together—a family, a life.

During that period, Apple reached a milestone of her own. While living in Orange County, she became a United States citizen—something she had worked toward patiently and with determination. It was a proud moment. After nearly twenty years in hospitality, including work with Marriott and Sandals, she chose to begin an entirely new chapter. She trained and became a professional massage therapist, dedicating herself to the craft with discipline and care. She was gifted at it. I was proud of her courage to reinvent herself.

Around the same time, something deeply personal resurfaced. I was contacted by the Italian consulate and informed that, due to an administrative failure years earlier, my Italian citizenship had quietly lapsed. Although I had renewed my passport multiple times, the underlying citizenship paperwork had never been properly restored after I became a U.S. citizen. When this was discovered, it shook me. Italy was not just a country to me—it was memory, blood, and origin. I returned to Italy, gathered proof of residency, and successfully regained my dual citizenship. As part of that process, and with my citizenship restored, I felt called to re-establish a physical connection to Italy. I identified a property in the Abruzzo region, where two families were living—the son and daughter of a cousin who had helped raise me as a child. That connection carried deep meaning, and I saw it as an opportunity to create a second residence—a place we could return to and share as part of our life together.

But what unfolded alongside that process was more revealing. Through a property dispute involving extended family—marked by deception and misplaced loyalty—I finally understood why my mother had left Italy in the first place. The pattern was not new; it was inherited. That realization brought peace rather than loss. I didn't need to reclaim Italy by owning it. I already carried it. Italy, I came to understand, is like a fine wine—best enjoyed in small, honest sips.

As life settled, awareness deepened. With Apple established in her new profession, I began to see more fully the life she had lived before me—growing up without parents, raised by grandparents, navigating adulthood without the stability most people take for granted. Over time, the role I occupied in her life resembled that of a guardian more than a mirrored partner. The recognition was steady and integrated. Love remained present. Alignment required examination. Apple will always be part of my life. That truth is clear.

What remains open is how to honor that bond while preserving reciprocity, equality, and shared direction.

Reflections

This chapter reflects leadership expressed through disciplined awareness.

Health becomes stewardship. Heritage becomes embodied identity. Travel becomes integration of history.

Marriage becomes conscious construction rather than momentum.

Perspective shifts from immersion to structural observation. Experience continues, yet pattern becomes visible.

Ancestry, partnership, finance, and identity integrate without dramatization.

Awareness stabilizes direction.

Key Takeaways

1. Discipline clarifies direction. When the body and mind are recalibrated, decision-making stabilizes.

2. Identity is internalized through lived integration. Heritage becomes embodied rather than possessed.

3. Mature leadership evaluates alignment continuously. Love, partnership, and shared direction require symmetry, not assumption.

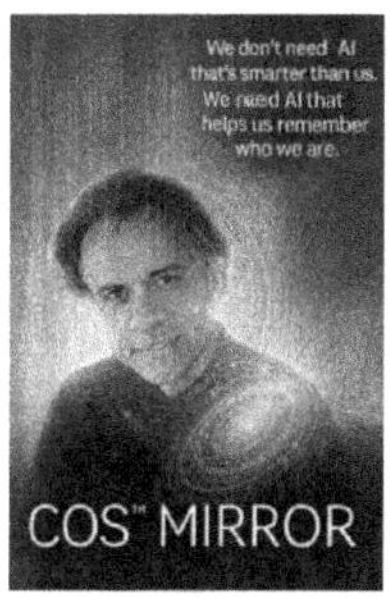

Q48

One more question. As you look ahead, what feels most meaningful to you now—and how does that shape how you understand life beyond this moment?

I believe life continues—not as personality or body, but as awareness shaped by experience. What is refined through living—insight, wisdom, discernment—does not disappear when the body rests. It carries forward because it has always existed. That continuity explains why meaning, philosophy, and truth resurface across cultures and generations in different forms. If I were given the choice to return, I would choose this life as I am now—carrying forward the awareness earned through experience. This lifetime has unfolded across eras of profound transformation: cultural, technological, and human. To witness that evolution—and to participate in it consciously—has been a privilege.

What feels significant now is the opportunity ahead. For the first time in history, humanity possesses tools capable of preserving and distributing wisdom at scale. Technology—

particularly AI—can serve as a reflective instrument. At its highest use, it mirrors human intelligence, refines insight, and extends access to clarity. Used consciously, it strengthens leadership, deepens self-awareness, and reduces unnecessary suffering by making wisdom more accessible.

That is what drives my work today. Through my writing, consulting, and the development of intelligent systems, I seek to share what I have learned—translating lived philosophy into frameworks others can apply. Precision matters. Service matters. Storytelling matters. Together, they allow transformation to be understood, embodied, and sustained. Technology can help carry intelligence forward. Awareness carries humanity forward.

Ultimately, what governs all of this is a higher intelligence—expressed through connection, coherence, and care. Another word for that intelligence is love. If awareness continues, it does so through that field.

And when I return, it will be in service to that continuity—with greater clarity, deeper compassion, and an expanded sense of responsibility.

Reflections

The final question shifts the narrative from biography to continuity.

The focus moves beneath events toward what endures through them. Awareness emerges as the throughline—expressed through lived recognition rather than abstract belief.

The perspective centers on stewardship: how insight is preserved, wisdom is translated, and how intelligence can be extended while honoring humanity.

Technology appears as an instrument—reflective, supportive, amplifying.

The arc completes quietly: life is framed as contribution.

What began as survival matures into service.

Key Takeaways

1. Awareness outlives circumstance. What is refined through experience becomes the true inheritance of a life.

2. Intelligence must remain human-centered. Tools extend capacity; responsibility remains human.

3. Legacy is stewardship. To live consciously is to carry wisdom forward—in systems, stories, and service.

This was my movie.

And it continues...

Three Things I Want You to Know

Before you move on, there are three things I want you to carry with you.

These come from everything you've just lived through with me—offered simply to support you as you continue on your own path.

1. Understand Who You Really Are

All I have to give you is the life I've lived thus far—the experiences that shaped me, the questions that guided me, and the understanding that emerged along the way. You can use it as a guide—something to reflect on as you shape your own path.

What I've learned is this: the most important thing in life is understanding the true nature of reality—and your place within it. From the very beginning of your life, stay curious. Ask real questions about the world you live in. Learn about the universe—the planets, the stars, the vastness of space. Ask yourself how it's possible that we are moving through an infinite cosmos at extraordinary speeds, yet everything remains in balance. Ask how life exists at all. Allow it to remain open, something to explore over time.

But if you stay curious long enough, you'll begin to recognize that there is an intelligence beyond what we can see— something that allows everything to exist, move, and sustain itself. Some people call it God. Others use different words. What matters is not the label, but the recognition that this unseen intelligence is real—because without it, nothing would be.

As you reflect on this, you'll begin to see that you are more than your body. Your body is made of cells. Those cells are made of elements that come from the same universe as the stars themselves. You are physically connected to everything around you. And then there are your thoughts, your inspirations, the quiet ideas that arrive without effort. Those do not come from muscle or bone. That's when you begin to understand: You are both a physical being and awareness itself—presence expressed through form, connected to something deeper. You are part of this greater intelligence—not separate from it.

As this understanding deepens, a natural question begins to take shape.

2. Discover Why You Are Here—and Respect Everyone Else's Journey

When you recognize that you are more than just a body, a natural question follows:

Why do I exist?

That question will stay with you for your entire life—and that's a good thing. For me, the answer became clear over time: I am here to express this intelligence through love, service, creativity, and contribution. That understanding shaped how I lived, worked, and related to others. Your answer may be different. And it will evolve.

Let it.

But here is what matters: Once you begin to understand *why* you are here, you must also understand that everyone else is on their own journey. No two paths are the same. You can inspire others. You can mentor, serve, and share what you've learned. But never expect others to see the world exactly as you do—or to grow at your pace. Respect their timing, lessons, and destination. When you truly understand who you are, why you are here, and that everyone else is walking their own path, something extraordinary happens naturally: You develop gratitude. Gratitude for being alive. Gratitude for awareness. Gratitude for the opportunity to experience this life at all.

That gratitude becomes a stabilizing force in how you live, choose, and move forward.

3. Lead Your Life—With Integrity and Wholeness

Once you understand who you are and carry gratitude for your existence, recognize that you are the leader of your life.

Leadership extends far beyond business or titles. It begins with how you live, choose, and align your actions with your values. You lead your personal life and relationships. You lead your work—whatever form that takes.

True leadership is integrated. It includes:

Your connection to Source—the unseen intelligence that sustains all life

Your cognition—the way you think, perceive, and understand

Your emotions—the way you feel, respond, and relate

Your social dimension—the relationships and connections you build

Your cultural dimension—the environments, systems, and world you influence.

When these elements are aligned, leadership becomes natural—I call it, Integrated Leadership Intelligence. It is something you come to embody through awareness and alignment.

Live with awareness of who you are, clarity about why you are here, respect for others' journeys, gratitude for existence, and responsibility for your life—and you will find your way.

That is all a father can hope to offer.

And One More Thing

There's one more thing I want to share with you.

After I finished this book, I found myself looking back—not just at the pages I had written, but at my life as a whole. Each of these answers could have become chapters in their own right. I lived them fully. I could have gone deeper. But what mattered most to me was capturing what was essential.

As I reflected, I noticed something that stopped me. I could see the arc of it more clearly. I began as a child carried from one country to another without understanding why. I learned to survive, to stabilize, and then to achieve. I built discipline, momentum, and a career. And then I collapsed under the weight of what I had not yet integrated.

From that collapse, I found something deeper—an inner intelligence that had always been present but unnamed. I gave it language and structure, building a philosophy around it. From it, I built companies and learned to love through it.

Then life tested it. Responsibility accumulated and isolation intensified. I stood at thresholds I never imagined I would face. And this time, I held differently. I observed, endured, and integrated. What began as survival matured into awareness. What began as ambition matured into stewardship. What began as searching matured into witnessing.

Only after living it did I see how coherent it all was. I've always been drawn to ways of understanding life that follow cycles—how things begin, unfold, and return. When I looked back at the moment I entered this world through that lens, I realized I was born at the very beginning of a cycle—one defined by growth, shedding, and quiet transformation.

Years later, without planning it or even being aware of it at the time, I found myself completing that same cycle just as I finished this work. I didn't set out to align it. I simply lived my life, followed what felt true, and did the work in front of me.

Only afterward did the pattern become visible. Moments like this have appeared throughout my life—subtle reminders of the relationship between what we experience and forces we do not immediately see.

When I look back now, I can see that my path unfolded with more intelligence than I could recognize while I was living it. That's why, from time to time, it helps to look at your life the way you'd watch a movie.

When you step back, you notice connections, timing, and meaning that aren't visible from inside the scene. You begin to see the arc—not just the moments.

That perspective brings understanding to the past and offers quiet guidance forward.

Reflection on Leadership

Across these forty-eight scenes, you have witnessed the arc of my life—from childhood in Italy to the present. What unfolds is not theory, but experience lived, tested, and integrated over time.

Leadership, as I've come to understand it, begins long before any title, role, or position. Leadership is who you are—and what you bring into the world. You carry that with you wherever you go, in whatever you choose to do. In that sense, you are always your own leader. I want to share with you how my own understanding of leadership developed, and how it can apply to your life.

When I look back, my leadership did not come from books or theories. It came from three passions that were formed very early in my life—especially during my first years growing up in Italy, a time when what I saw around me quietly shaped who I was becoming.

The first was mathematics. I loved its precision. The clarity. The way problems could be understood, broken down, and solved step by step. It taught me to think clearly and methodically, and to respect structure.

The second was hospitality. I grew up watching my mother work in a café, serving people with care, warmth, and pride. From her, I learned that excellence lives in how you treat people. Service, when done with intention, becomes a form of leadership.

The third was storytelling. I learned early on that every moment in life can become a story. When you look back, your life reveals itself as a narrative. And how you show up in each moment determines the story you are living—whether you realize it or not.

Those three passions stayed with me throughout my life. They became my drivers. They shaped how I worked, how I led, and how I related to the world.

Over time, I realized that these passions naturally came together in a simple way: *inner science* and *outer excellence*, expressed through a life story.

As my career evolved, and as I worked with people, teams, and organizations of all kinds, I began to see patterns. I started mapping the different parts of who we are—not just as leaders at work, but as human beings in life.

At its core, it begins within.

Everything starts with what I consider the Source—your philosophy. How you see reality. Who you believe you are. Whether you see yourself only as a human being, or as part of something larger—an infinite intelligence that connects the seen and unseen. This Source is where creativity, purpose, and meaning come from. For me, this is my Creative Optimum Self—the foundation of everything I do.

Over time, I came to understand that when this philosophy is lived inwardly—through awareness, presence, and alignment—it operates as Integrated Being Intelligence, and when it is expressed outwardly—through action, relationships, and responsibility—it becomes Integrated Leadership Intelligence.

From there, leadership requires emotional maturity—your own first, and then the capacity to support it in others. Life teaches you that not everyone sees the world the same way, and not everyone is on the same journey. Learning patience, compassion, and emotional maturity becomes essential. This is emotional intelligence.

Once you can ground yourself emotionally, you begin to think more clearly. You learn how to solve problems, design systems, and manage complexity—whether that's in your personal life or in large projects involving many people. This is where the precision I learned from mathematics shows up as cognitive intelligence. Then comes the ability to build bridges—to inspire others and align people around shared goals. To work as a team rather than as individuals pulling in different directions.

Over time, this expands into understanding cultures, environments, and systems—how people work together, and how organizations function. This becomes social and cultural intelligence. When all of these elements are working together—your inner awareness, emotional maturity, clear thinking, and how you relate to others—leadership becomes integrated. It moves beyond something you switch on and off—it becomes how you live.

When I look at my own life, I can see these elements clearly. A Source philosophy that guides me. The ability to manage emotions. Clear thinking and structure. Meaningful relationships. And a sense of responsibility for the world I participate in and serve. These are the "dials" I continue to adjust and refine—personally and professionally—to stay balanced and productive.

As you embark on your own journey, what matters most is discovering what drives *you*. For me, it was mathematics, hospitality, and storytelling. For you, it may be something entirely different.

Once you understand what truly moves you, build around it. Ask yourself who you are, why you are here, and what kind of life you want to live.

Learn how to manage yourself first—your emotions, your thoughts, your awareness—and then learn how to engage with the world around you with intention and care.

This is a practice—one that unfolds across a lifetime.

Stay curious. Stay balanced.

And always remain aware of how you are living the story that will one day be told.

Leadership is something you live and practice—every day, in every role, with every choice you make.

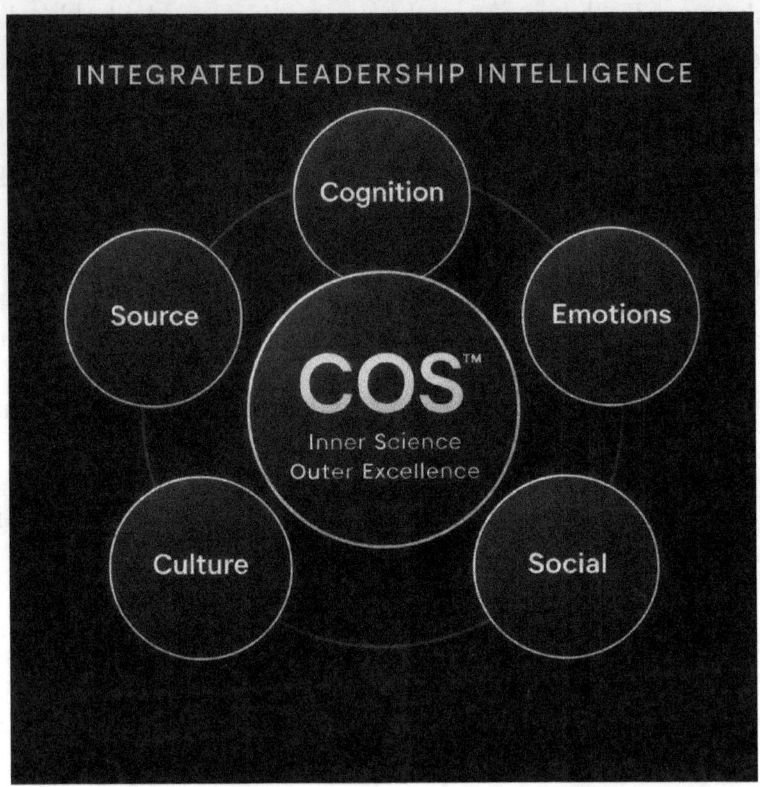

Source • Cognition • Emotions • Social • Culture

When these dimensions operate in coherence, the Creative Optimum Self expresses through leadership.

The Architecture Revealed

In the Author's Note, I shared that the Reflections provide context—naming the patterns, pressures, and internal shifts that shaped each moment—while the Key Takeaways accumulate over time, gradually revealing the arc of Integrated Leadership Intelligence.

Leadership began for me long before I had language for it. It appeared first as responsibility. Then as protection. Then as discipline. Then as repair. Later, it became authorship. Eventually, stewardship.

If you step back now—after experiencing these forty-eight scenes with me—you may begin to observe the gradual integration of five dimensions that were always present—at times balanced, at times strained, yet always active.

Everything began with Source.

As a child in Italy. As an immigrant. As a son. As a young man sitting alone after loss. Meaning remained my first instinct. Even before strategy or reaction, a quiet question would arise:

what does this mean?

who am I within this moment?

That inner philosophy guided me long before I named it the Creative Optimum Self.

It became the invisible anchor across chaos, ambition, grief, and reinvention.

Then came awareness through the body.

The surgery as a child. The blood pressure on Wall Street. The exhaustion during caregiving. The weight gained. The weight released. The body reflected alignment and misalignment with precision. When ignored, it spoke louder. When heard, it recalibrated. Leadership is lived through the nervous system.

Alongside that, the Cognition dimension strengthened. My training in mathematics, my work in banking, and years inside complex organizations refined how I think. I learned to navigate complexity and design order. That capacity became one of my strongest tools. Yet cognition alone required alignment. When it moved ahead, pressure surfaced elsewhere. When it served Source, it amplified clarity.

The Social dimension matured through relationships and institutions. Through family, colleagues, clients, marriage, mentors, and the organizations I served, I came to understand leadership as relational before positional. Trust was built, tested, at times fractured, and rebuilt again. Responsibility is carried in how we show up for others—listening, bridging differences, remaining steady when reciprocity thins. Influence rooted in coherence endures. Influence detached from identity fades.

Woven through it all was Culture. I was born in Italy and shaped in America. Immigration offered perspective before language formed around it. I carried heritage in my heart, while my life expanded through global experience—work, travel, responsibility, and reinvention. Returning to Italy later in life became a way of honoring where I began while recognizing how much broader I had become. Culture gave depth, sensitivity, and memory. Travel expanded my lens. Each place left something within me.

Over time, I came to see myself as shaped by many worlds—grounded in heritage, enriched by experience, and guided by universal principles of responsibility, dignity, coherence, and love. Across the seven chapters, these five dimensions did not mature in symmetry. Each carried different weight across different seasons. Ambition strengthened cognition. Crisis pressed against the body. Culture resurfaced through ancestry and memory. Social systems expanded, fractured, and reformed as relationships evolved.

Through it all, a pattern quietly revealed itself: When Source remained steady, the other dimensions organized naturally around it. As alignment drifted, pressure surfaced elsewhere. When coherence stabilizes inwardly—when awareness, alignment, and philosophy organize the inner world—it becomes Integrated Being Intelligence. It is how intelligence lives within you.

When that same coherence expresses outwardly—through decisions, relationships, responsibility, and execution—it becomes Integrated Leadership Intelligence. It is how intelligence moves through you into the world. The Source remains constant. The expression matures. Integrated Leadership Intelligence is about understanding the interplay between dimensions. It is conscious adjustment—recognizing how survival, achievement, collapse, love, grief, and reinvention all participate in integration.

By the time you reach the final chapter—Becoming the Witness—identity begins to separate from circumstance. Awareness expands beyond collapse.

Integrated Leadership Intelligence stabilizes from within.

That is the arc—

Endurance becomes capability.
Capability becomes authorship.
Authorship becomes service.
Service becomes stewardship.

This architecture offers a lens—a way to understand how a life organizes across dimensions, and how meaning, body, cognition, relationships, and culture interact and balance over time.

Every life carries structure. Every life forms patterns. Some are examined. Some are simply lived.

What matters is that integration is possible—that coherence can be cultivated when awareness guides expression.

Leadership is integration unfolding across a lifetime.

My invitation is to become aware of awareness—and to do it consciously by watching your own movie in real time.

Final Note

As I complete this book, I want to leave you with this understanding.

Creative Optimum Self is my living philosophy.

In my companion volume, *Creative Optimum Self: Transform Your Life and Your World*, I share how this philosophy was developed through deep reflection and inspiration from life and business principles, and architected into the Inner and Outer Steps.

This is a living practice and a never-ending journey. As you apply the Inner Steps faithfully, you evolve and are guided to execute the Outer Steps intuitively. You begin to see your life with greater clarity.

You become more aware of how you think, how you feel, and how you respond.

You become aware of awareness itself. In that awareness, you become the witness and live as Integrated Being Intelligence.

From this state, your inner awareness expresses itself outwardly through Source, cognition, emotions, social connection, and cultural expansion—naturally embodying Integrated Leadership Intelligence.

And from there, life continues to unfold—expanding, refining, and evolving through every moment.

Thirteen COS Questions

Over the years, through coaching, reflection, and deep personal inquiry, I began returning to the same set of questions—not only for myself, but with clients, leaders, and individuals at pivotal moments in their lives.

These questions are simple, sensory, and deeply human. They invite you to notice the preferences, memories, and experiences that quietly shape you. When answered honestly, they reveal patterns—signals of identity, taste, values, and meaning that often live beneath roles, expectations, and noise.

In this way, they become a form of orientation. They help you see yourself more clearly and begin shaping a narrative around who you are and how you move through the world.

What follows are my own answers.

1. What is your favorite sandwich?

Two slices of sourdough bread with Italian hot pepper sauce, burrata, prosciutto, fresh basil, and sun-dried tomatoes.

2. What is your favorite fruit?

Blackberries.

3. What is your favorite drink?

Fresh coconut water.

4.   What was your first concert?

Neil Diamond at the Spectrum in Philly—open stage, incredible energy, and an unforgettable night.

5.   What is your favorite automobile?

BMW.

6.   Who is your favorite movie character?

James Bond.

7.   What is your favorite sound?

Silence—the space where everything becomes clear.

8.   What is your favorite song?

Shame by Evelyn "Champagne" King—it always makes me want to dance.

9.   What is your favorite fabric?

Cashmere.

10. What is your favorite smell?

Jasmine.

11. Who is your favorite singer?

Lionel Richie and Malika Ayane—an expression of my dual heritage.

12. Who is your favorite actor?

Robert Redford.

13. What do you think happens when the body dies?

The body dissolves, as it has been doing all along through regeneration.

Awareness—wisdom, presence, consciousness—remains.

It has always been here and will continue.

What these answers reveal is simple: the small details of our lives carry meaning. The foods we enjoy, the music that moves us, the textures, sounds, and stories we return to—each reflects something about how we experience the world.

When you pause to notice these preferences, patterns begin to emerge. They help you understand your sensibilities, your memories, and the environments where you feel most alive.

In that sense, these questions invite you to observe your life more closely—to recognize the signals shaping your identity and the narrative you are living.

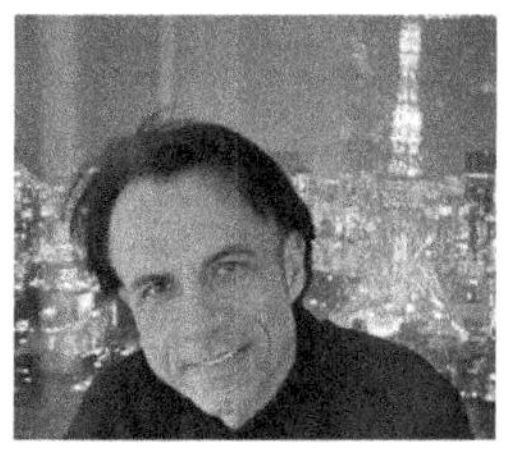

About the Author

Costantino Delli is a leadership architect, coach, author, and founder of the COS (Creative Optimum Self) Philosophy—an integrated system uniting Integrated Being Intelligence and Integrated Leadership Intelligence. His work bridges inner mastery with operational excellence, helping individuals and leaders integrate who they are with how they think, decide, act, and serve.

Born in Taranto, Italy, Delli immigrated to the United States at the age of eight. Early experiences shaped by hospitality, mathematics, storytelling, and adversity formed the foundation of a philosophy grounded in precision, empathy, and human-centered responsibility.

Delli began his career in finance and systems engineering, working across banking, defense analytics, and global financial markets, where precision, reliability, and disciplined execution became foundational to his leadership philosophy. A professional and personal breakdown became the catalyst for the inner transformation that would shape his life's work.

Over time, Delli articulated the Creative Optimum Self, integrating inner awareness with creative expression and disciplined execution. From this foundation emerged two complementary expressions of the same intelligence: Integrated Being Intelligence, which describes how intelligence is lived internally through awareness, embodiment, and presence, and Integrated Leadership Intelligence, which describes how that same intelligence is expressed externally through thinking, relating, organizing, and serving in the world. Together, they form one coherent system expressed across dimensions: being and doing, inner and outer, awareness and application.

He founded COS 4 Excellence, advising organizations across finance, media, and technology on leadership architecture, enterprise transformation, and integrated human–system performance. He later extended the COS framework through COS AI Mirror—a proprietary conscious framework enabling leaders and organizations to develop intelligence aligned with their values, voice, and lived wisdom. Over the course of his career, Delli has worked across finance, technology, media, entertainment, healthcare, and consulting, contributing to the design and transformation of complex systems and advising leaders in environments where clarity, trust, and performance are inseparable. Across all expressions, his work remains guided by the COS Philosophy—one intelligence, lived fully, within and without.

Delli's first book, *The Way: Live Your Dream, It's Not a Secret!*—now evolved into *Creative Optimum Self: Transform Your Life and Your World*—introduced a framework of five inner and five outer steps for service and leadership excellence. His second book, *48 Answers for My Son: An Architecture of Integrated Leadership Intelligence*, expresses the lived architecture of leadership, responsibility, and execution through reflection and experience.

He currently resides in California.

Return to the Foundation

48 Answers for My Son expresses leadership through lived experience—a cinematic journey of decisions, discipline, responsibility, and integration.

For the inner framework that anchors this architecture, return to:

Creative Optimum Self: Transform Your Life and Your World

Inner awareness and outer expression are one intelligence, lived inwardly and expressed outwardly as a unified way of being.

Future works will explore how the Creative Optimum Self can be cultivated in education, integrated into the workplace, and applied to broader social challenges.

A portion of the net proceeds from this book supports the development of COS 4 LIFE, a mission dedicated to fostering Loving, Inspiring, Fulfilling Existence—personally and collectively.

Because when individuals awaken their Creative Optimum Self, communities strengthen, leadership matures, and meaningful change becomes possible.

Learn more: www.cosphilosophy.com